RUSSIA AND
POSTMODERN
DETERRENCE

Selected Books by Stephen J. Cimbala

Clausewitz and Chaos: Friction in War and Military Policy
Military Persuasion in War and Policy: The Power of Soft
Mysteries of the Cold War (Policy Studies Organisational Series)
Nuclear Strategizing: Deterrence and Reality
Nuclear Deterrence and Arms Control: A New Century
Politics of Warfare
Russia and Armed Persuasion
Shield of Dreams: Missile Defenses and Nuclear Strategy
The U.S., NATO, and Military Burden-sharing

RUSSIA AND POSTMODERN DETERRENCE

MILITARY POWER AND ITS CHALLENGES FOR SECURITY

STEPHEN J. CIMBALA

AND PETER RAINOW

Potomac Books, Inc.
Washington, D.C.

Library of Congress Cataloging-in-Publication Data

Cimbala, Stephen J.
Russia and postmodern deterrence : military power and its challenges for security / Stephen J. Cimbala and Peter Rainow.
p. cm.
Includes bibliographical references and index.
ISBN-13: 978-1-57488-813-3 (hardcover : alk. paper)
ISBN-10: 1-57488-813-7 (hardcover : alk. paper)
1. Russia (Federation)—Military policy. 2. National security—Russia (Federation) 3. Nuclear weapons—Russia (Federation) 4. Deterrence (Strategy) I. Rainow, Peter Jacob. II. Title.
UA770.C5626 2006
355.02'17—dc22

2006017772

Printed in the United States of America on acid-free paper that meets the American National Standards Institute Z39-48 Standard.

Potomac Books, Inc.
22841 Quicksilver Drive
Dulles, Virginia 20166

First Edition

10 9 8 7 6 5 4 3 2 1

CONTENTS

ACKNOWLEDGMENTS

Grateful acknowledgment is made by the authors to Stephen J. Blank and David M. Glantz for encouragement and support for research on Soviet and Russian military topics. We also gratefully acknowledge Penn State University-Delaware County for administrative support, and Rick Russell and Michie Shaw of Potomac Books, Inc., for their interest in and support for this project.

Finally, we thank our families for their love, patience, and support.

INTRODUCTION

Using the terms "Russia" and "postmodern" in the same sentence might make many western analysts and writers blanch. Russia is in many ways a post-communist country struggling to adapt to the modern world economically and politically. But the use of postmodern as an adjective to describe some of the problems of deterrence that face Russia in the twenty-first century is not inappropriate. Postmodernism is a set of social, cultural, and political traits. For Russia's political leaders and military planners, a postmodern setting is defined by the following realities:

- The world's leading military and economic powers, with one exception, are market economies and political democracies.
- The Revolution in Military Affairs (RMA), based on advances in information, electronics, and communications, is driving both civil and military technology innovation.
- The "realities" of the Cold War era, including deterrence based on nuclear weapons and on conventional armed forces organized and trained for massive wars of attrition, have changed.

The implications of each of these points for future Russian strategy and policymaking are profound.

The first, which describes the nature of the great power states in the early decades of the twenty-first century, essentially refers to NATO and China. NATO is not truly a state but rather an alliance, but it is not an alliance of equals. The NATO alliance's leading member, the United States, is now the only state capable of both global nuclear and conventional military power projection. As the U.S. wars in Afghanistan in 2001 and Iraq in 2003 have demonstrated, the U.S. military reach is effectively without limit. In this projection of U.S. power—even as Russia "cooperated" with U.S. intervention in Afghanistan against terrorism and did not object to American and allied bases in neighboring former Soviet states—influential Russian political and military figures warned of the dangers of a permanent American military presence in the region.

In the post-Soviet era, Russia perceives that its enormous territorial space and resulting vast geopolitical defense perimeter requires the capability for deterrence of attacks from any quarter. Potential threats to Russian space include neighboring states torn by civil strife, a NATO expanded to some twenty-six members, and still others who seek to increase the economic and political distance between themselves and Russia's current regime. Russian influence over what we might describe as the "security space" adjacent to the country's borders can be expected to contract over the next decade or so even if there is no shooting war on its periphery. In addition, inside Russia's own territory, its military and other security forces are hard-pressed to maintain order against rebels in Chechnya. Russia has fought two wars there in less than a decade (the second is still in progress), and the prospects for a solution much beyond the Roman manner of dealing with Carthage remain remote.

The second reality—RMA and its implications for Russia—is closely related to the first. Russia must, if it is to remain in the ranks of great powers, move away from the mass conscript army of its communist past to a smaller, voluntary, and technology-leveraging force that is properly paid, equipped, motivated, and trained for conflicts of the type that Russia will most likely face in the future.[1] Russia recognizes that it is far behind the West in leveraging modern technology for military purposes. Therefore, Russia's current military doctrine explicitly relies on nuclear weapons as its first line of deterrence against *either* nuclear or conventional military attack. Stephen J. Blank has summarized,

> Thus the Security Concept appears to declare the concept of limited nuclear war as Moscow's official war strategy against a variety of contingencies, and it further reflects Russia's interest in using tactical nuclear weapons as actual war fighting weapons. Key officials have confirmed that limited nuclear war is Russia's officially acknowledged strategy for many different contingencies. This strategy also reflects Moscow's bizarre, unsettling, and unprecedented belief that Russia—despite forty years of Soviet experience to the contrary—would be able to control nuclear escalation and nuclear war as long as Russia was the initiator.[2]

In addition, Russia's conventional military weakness means that it (in contrast to the United States and NATO) cannot project power far beyond its borders without relying on nuclear threats. To extricate itself from this doctrinal dead end or strategic straitjacket, Russia must not only move both its economy and its military into the information age, it must also rethink of the very concept of military service that Russia inherited from the Soviet Union.

The third point noted—changed geopolitical and strategic realities—emphasizes the new world order in which Russia finds itself and especially the implications of the new geopolitical structure for Russia's policy options. The simple bipolar world of the Cold War is gone. Russia must now deal with a "multiplex" international system defined by

- a dominant U.S. economic and military actor that has an officially nonhostile relationship with Russia but still points its nuclear missiles primarily at targets located on Russian territory (and vice versa)
- a China that aspires to overtake Russia (at least) as the world's putative second ranked military power, including hegemony over the Pacific basin and the capability to project air and maritime power well beyond its own state borders
- an assertive NATO that has momentarily paused in the process of enlarging its membership with former Soviet states, but which has given Russia no promissory note or veto against future enlargement, for example, to include Ukraine
- the restive Central Asia and Caucasian regions, replete with western powers that are interested in Caspian Basin oil reserves, dissatisfied Islamic separatists brewing dissidence in Chechnya and elsewhere, and ethno-national unrest always simmering beneath the surface or exploding above it in Georgia and Armenia and in the Central Asian "Stans" that serve as Russia's southern security glacis
- the possible emergence of viable and deployable technologies for theater or even national missile defense within the first two decades of the new century, and the possibility of American unilateral predominance in this regard.

In short, Russia confronts a radically new political and military world order that demands movement from modern into postmodern thinking about deterrence and defense. If we follow the typology of Charles C. Moskos in order to distinguish some of the important attributes of modern from postmodern militaries, using the U.S. military, Table 1 is instructive.

Table 1: U.S. Armed Forces in Three Eras

Variable	Modern (Pre-Cold War) 1900–1945	Late Modern (Cold War) 1945–1990	Postmodern (Post-Cold War) Since 1990
Perceived threat	Enemy invasion	Nuclear war	Subnational (ethnic violence, terrorism)
Force structure	Mass army, conscription	Large professional army	Small professional army
Major mission definition	Defense of homeland	Support of alliance	New missions (peacekeeping, humanitarian)
Dominant military professional	Combat leader	Manager or technician	Soldier-statesman; Soldier-scholar
Public attitude toward military	Supportive	Ambivalent	Indifferent

Source: Excerpted from Charles C. Moskos, "Toward a Postmodern Military: The United States as a Paradigm," Ch. 2, in Moskos, John Allen Williams, and David R. Segal, eds., *The Postmodern Military: Armed Forces after the Cold War* (New York: Oxford University Press, 2000), 14–31, citation from table, on page 15. This is not the complete table and Moskos is not responsible for its use here.

Obviously, one cannot proceed directly from the American version of this matrix to a Russian equivalent. Even this version of it could change in the aftermath of 9/11 and the new priorities placed on defense of the American homeland. For Russian and Soviet leaders past and present, the definition of a primary political and military objective in the modern, late modern, and postmodern eras has been self-evident. Defense of the homeland supersedes all else. The reasons for this priority include:

- Russia's history of invasion and attack from hostile neighbors
- the yin and yang of Russian imperial and Soviet expansion that pushed borders outward against resistant military competitors
- the near death experience in the aftermath of Germany's invasion in 1941 and its military lessons as seen by Soviet and Russian planners
- the Cold War vulnerability of the Soviet Union (as well as the United States) to nuclear annihilation if the two nuclear superpowers had decided to engage their most destructive weapons

- the authoritarian political systems of Russian and Soviet vintage that relied on a truncated policymaking process mired in suspicion and paranoia, including inflated threat assessments and voracious demands from armed forces for shares of the national economic product.

Russia today is not Upper Volta with missiles but is a medium power instead of a great power without its large nuclear arsenal and long-range delivery systems. These weapons of mass destruction (WMD) keep Russia politically visible among self-proclaimed great powers but only at a considerable price. Nuclear weapons are a vanishing deterrent in the face of technology challenges: first, from high-technology conventional warfare, resting on capabilities for long-range precision strike, stealth, and C4ISR (command, control, communications, computers, intelligence, surveillance, and reconnaissance); second, from antimissile defense systems that might permit a state to deny another state its retaliatory strike, thus permitting the first state to launch a nuclear attack with impunity. Even if antinuclear defenses do not overturn the nuclear revolution based on assured retaliation, they may be good enough to provide theater missile defenses that support U.S. and allied military power projection against Russia's perceived interests.

Russia, in short, faces a postmodern world and therefore has a postmodern deterrence and defense problem:

1. The international system has changed from the simplicity of the bipolar Cold War system into the complexity of a uni-multipolarity, with the United States in a predominant position on security matters; Russia has room to leverage this system in favorable directions, but it must make a number of difficult decisions in economic and security policy in order to do so.

2. Globalization has forced states to choose between involvement and participation in the new international order, either by opening their borders to cultural influence and empowering new elites in business and government or by dropping from the ranks of aspiring major regional or global powers; a sick Russian economy in the twenty-first century will reduce the interest of West European democracies in integrating Russia into a larger northern security community.

3. As a result of numbers 1 and 2, Russia must transform its military into a force that is more professional, democratically accountable, and capable of organizational reform to take advantage of the post-industrial Revolution in Military

Affairs. This new military, compared to its immediate predecessor in the first decade after the Cold War, will be lighter,
more mobile and flexible in composition, and less reliant on
coercion as opposed to shared professional values in relations between officers and enlisted personnel.

To accomplish these things, Russia will need a state that works. A
"state that works" implies a public order that can adhere to the law
by the most powerful forces in society. It also implies that a
policymaking process will begin to develop that brings together interest groups and government in a matrix not dependent on corruption
and kleptocracy. Russia can have neither a postmodern economy nor
a postmodern military if it lacks a modern polity. Only Russians can
introduce a modern polity that expects political efficacy on the part
of citizens and enforces legal restraints on the political absolutism
that has marked Russia's turbulent history since Ivan the Terrible.
Without that, Russia's armed forces will be politically adrift, economically shortchanged, and professionally corrupt. Most important, they
will unable to defend the state in good time.

In this book, general themes are followed up in specific chapter
studies. In chapter 1, we consider the problem of surprise attack as
one of Russia's and the Soviet Union's historical and contemporary
preoccupations. Post–Cold War Russia may seem to have no realistic
fear on this score. NATO has neither the intent nor a plan to attack
Russia. Russians have objected to NATO enlargement after the Cold
War, but this is more of a political embarrassment than a realistic
military threat. NATO expansion to include Poland, Hungary, and the
Czech Republic in 1999 coincided with the alliance's air war against
Yugoslavia over Russian objections. But NATO's eastward political
thrust is a two-edged military proposition. NATO must extend its security guarantee over more territory, which makes any NATO invasion into Russia harder, not easier (because of a diminishing strength
gradient from NATO's military pivot in western Europe toward its
eastern perimeter).

But NATO is not Russia's only concern near its borders. Instability in the former Soviet states in Central Asia and the Caucasus
caused Russia to deploy peacekeeping forces in its "near abroad" in
the 1990s. In the same decade, war in Chechnya also plagued the
Russian leadership with the threat of secession. The U.S.–Russian
cooperation against terrorism after 9/11 is good news for Russia (allowing Putin to depict his campaign in Chechnya as part of a global
antiterrorism mission) and bad news (opening former Soviet states in
Central Asia to U.S. bases and other influences). China and Russia

have a politically favorable relationship and a brisk arms trade, but they also share a large border along some slightly populated Russian territory. Russia also observed U.S. success in ousting the regime of Saddam Hussein in Iraq and pondered the likelihood of other American military interventions in the Middle East. Given this range of possible scenarios, Russia does well to consult its past experience in this century with strategic military surprise, especially that which occurred with Germany's invasion in June 1941.

There is a great deal of talk in current U.S. military circles about military transformation. Russia, given its geographical immensity, historical vulnerability to invasion, and periodic outbursts of imperialism has dealt with more than one transformation in military technology, military organization, or military art. The Russian art of war is now undergoing another test in the "post-post Cold War" world of the twenty-first century. In chapter 2, we revisit a modern case of Russian military transformation that is not always recognized as such— Soviet political and military adaptation to the nuclear revolution. The advent of nuclear weapons demanded rethinking of the Marxian catechism about war and history and required a reexamination of all aspects of Soviet military art and science. An assessment of this past transformation may hold clues about the probable success or failure of Russians now faced with transformation of another kind.

Postmodern Russia seeks to modernize its military and move beyond the nuclear dependency of the Cold War. But until it can catch up with post–Desert Storm conventional high-technology weapons of the kind deployed by the United States and NATO, Russia must rely on its nuclear deterrent, which now covers more possible scenarios than during the Cold War. Russia's nuclear doctrine avers that a nuclear response might be appropriate not only under conditions of nuclear attack but also in cases of conventional warfare waged against Russian territory or near its territory and threatening to Russia. Whereas the Cold War Soviets were assumed to have conventional military superiority over NATO, the post–Cold War Russians are inferior to the West in non-nuclear capabilities.

Although a replay of Barbarossa by an expanded NATO is not likely, cautious Russian military planners must now expect to rely on nuclear "first use" for deterrence and for dealing with any outbreak of inadvertent war. This excessive tasking of Russia's nuclear deterrent is worrisome, as chapter 3 explains, because Russia's nuclear command and control system is unpredictable. The entire complex of C3I (command, control, communications, and intelligence, to which many now add a fourth "C" for computers) supporting Russia's nuclear deterrent is subject to considerable doubt by western observers and by some Russians. Problems of decayed equipment, uncertain arrangements for delegation of nuclear authority, and possibly flawed political expectations in a crisis could lead to mistakes in alerting forces or even a preemptive attack.

In chapter 4, we consider the implications of the U.S. decision to scrap the Anti-Ballistic Missile (ABM) Treaty of 1972 and to move toward eventual deployment of national missile defenses (NMD). This relates peripherally to the question of military surprise attack. The Soviets feared during the Cold War that U.S. technology would create a breakthrough in missile defenses that would counter Russia's deterrent. We now know that such a quantum leap in missile defense technology did not occur in the 1980s or even the 1990s. But the United States continued research and development on missile defenses in the 1990s, and the U.S. Congress by 1999 had shoved President Clinton nearly all the way toward a commitment to deploy NMD. Predictably, President George W. Bush decided in December 2001 to move beyond the ABM Treaty. Russia's President Putin offered only a muted reaction to the decision because his focus had moved on to Russian foreign policy, which he wanted to more closely reflect that of NATO and the European Union. Chapter 4 considers some of the implications of U.S. missile defenses for Russia in the context of almost inevitable, albeit regrettable, nuclear weapons spread.

Russia shares with the United States an interest in preventing the spread of nuclear weapons and long-range delivery systems to additional world leaders with revisionist political objectives. Additionally, in the aftermath of the 9/11 attacks on U.S. soil, the United States and Russia have asserted a community of interest in deterring terrorist attacks as well as breaking up the most threatening terrorist organizations worldwide. In chapter 5, we consider the problem of nuclear weapons spread from theoretical and policy perspectives. We first review some of the contending arguments between optimists and pessimists about nuclear proliferation: optimists think the international system can withstand additional and significant amounts of proliferation, provided that anti-status quo states or nonstate leaders can be kept away from nuclear and other WMD and ballistic or other delivery systems. Pessimists about proliferation maintain that the world is not as logically structured or as hierarchically determined as is the international system as depicted by realists. Although proliferation-permissive realists make some elegant theoretical points, their policy-relevant prescriptions are unconvincing. Nor is any United States–Russia alignment against proliferation guaranteed. Russia wants to sell weapons for hard currency, and its military-industrial complex is suspect for having leaked nuclear weapons-grade materials, as well as scientific and technical know-how. In regard to weapons sales, the United States can perhaps mitigate but not eliminate the incentives and consequences. To stop knowledge leaks, the United States has already funded some cooperative security programs to retrain Russian scientists for nonmilitary research and has helped Russia improve the safety and security of its stored weapons.

Despite its understandable concern about being left behind in the military-technical revolution of the late twentieth and early twenty-first centuries, Russia has faced a low-technology but high-intensity battlefront since the end of the Soviet Union. Its peacekeeping forces have deployed to various Caucasian and Central Asian states formerly included in the Soviet empire. Most important, the Russian army has been tasked to pacify rebellious Chechnya twice since the end of the Cold War. The first Russo–Chechen war fought by post–Cold War Russia ended in political stalemate in 1996 after two years of fighting. It was a great military embarrassment for Russia, some reasons for which are discussed in chapter 6. Russia's military was sent into Chechnya in 1994 with hastily laid plans, poorly motivated and prepared troops, underequipped forces, and ambivalent commanders lacking in a clear sense of mission or purpose.

In 1999, Russia tried again. The Putin administration has pursued the anti-Chechen campaign with more relentless vigor and less apparent willingness to compromise than did the Yeltsin administration. Nevertheless, Russia shares with the United States a military zeitgeist that is more attuned to large-scale conventional war than it is to conducting counterterror operations and low-intensity conflicts. The U.S. experience in Afghanistan in 2001 does not necessarily contradict this assertion, considering how the American approach to that conflict minimized the use of U.S. ground forces and used airpower and advanced technology to maximum advantage.

THE GHOST OF BARBAROSSA:
AVOIDING SURPRISE ATTACK

Russia has inherited from the former Soviet Union a rich tapestry of political and military thought that is highly nuanced. It is grounded in Soviet historical experience and connected to the ideological prism through which the Communist Party of the Soviet Union saw the world. High in importance for the Soviet military from the end of the Second World War until the collapse of Lenin's experiment in 1991 was the avoidance of a decisive surprise attack in the first phase or "initial period" of war. A repeat of the disastrous Soviet experience against the German Wehrmacht in the early stages of Operation Barbarossa, Hitler's invasion of Russia in June 1941, could not be tolerated.

The Soviet experience with, and theory for, dealing with the initial period of war is still hardwired into the brains of Russia's General Staff and Ministry of Defense. Beyond that, Russia in the early twenty-first century casts a small military shadow compared with the Soviet Union of the Cold War years. Russia faces possible security dilemmas on multiple points of the compass. Unlike the Soviet Union, however, Russia's imminent military challenges are not the risks of involvement in a possible world war. Instead, Russia confronts a new world disorder of border conflicts, insurgency, terrorism, and stability operations all calling for military transformation of its Soviet-style Armageddon mentality into something lighter, faster, and more professional. Incidents like Barbarossa come in small as well as in larger packages.

The Great Patriotic War
Russian military historians have carefully studied the time from the commencement of hostilities until friendly forces are within grasp of their initial operational and strategic military objectives. They refer

to this expanse of time as the "initial period of war."[1] The authoritative study by General of the Army S. P. Ivanov on this subject,
published in 1974, was part of a broader interest within the Soviet
military establishment in the problem of threat assessment and the
avoidance of surprise attack.[2] Having turned away from the one vari-
ant war model of the Khrushchev years, Soviet military planners
reviewed their World War II experience in strategic operations conducted by several *fronts* in a continental theater of operations.[3] Those
studies revealed the strengths and weaknesses of the Soviet conduct
of campaigns at the operational and strategic levels in the early
period of the war and subsequently. After World War II, Soviet commanders would succeed only if they considered a different technology and policy context. Special account would have to be taken of
the "revolution in military affairs" that had occurred by developing
and deploying nuclear weapons.[4]

According to Lt. Gen. M. M. Kir'yan, the initial period of war is
"the time during which the belligerents fought with previously deployed groupings of armed forces to achieve the immediate tactical
goals or to create advantageous conditions for committing the main
forces to battle and for conducting subsequent operations."[5] Maj.
Gen. M. Cherednichenko noted in a 1961 article that prior to the
Second World War, the initial period of war was defined in Soviet
military theory according to World War I experience. This meant,
according to Cherednichenko, the period from the official declara-
tion of war and the start of social mobilization to the beginning of
main battle force engagements.[6] Soviet planners, following this
model, assumed that covering forces deployed in the border military
districts were to fight the first phases of the defensive battle. Their
mission was to cause attrition of enemy forces and to delay the enemy advance until the Soviet second echelon forces counterattacked.
However, during intermediate years, the widespread introduction into
the armed forces of tanks, aviation, and other means of armed conflict "revealed a strong possibility of surprise offensives and the
achievement of decisive aims at the beginning of war."[7]

Kir'yan's article in the June 1988 *Military-Historical Journal*
notes that Soviet military theory during the 1930s taught that a surprise attack with already mobilized forces could "give the expected
results only against a small state" and that, for an offensive against
the Soviet Union, a definite time of mobilization, concentration, and
deployment of the German main forces would be required.[8] Soviet
military analysts have charged the political and armed forces leadership on the eve of war with strategic errors in addition to theoretical ones. Failures to assess warning intelligence accurately and

reluctance of the political leadership to take sensible preparatory measures in the western border districts of the USSR allowed Soviet defenders to fall below viable standards for readiness. This indictment of the Soviet armed forces High Command and of Stalin personally was offered by A. M. Nekrich in his classic *1941 22 Iyunya* (22 June 1941).[9]

Studies by western specialists on the Soviet armed forces have supported much of Nekrich's verdict, if not all of his analyses in detail. John Erickson has noted the effects on the proficiency of Soviet command in the early stages of World War II of Stalin's purges of the armed forces' leadership from 1937 to 1939.[10] Much of the prewar theory of deep operations and mechanized motorized warfare, which had been pioneered in Soviet professional military writing of the 1920s and 1930s, was forgotten in the aftermath of the military purges only to be relearned in the hasty reorganization of Soviet defenses after June 22, 1941.

Misinterpretation of the experience of the Spanish Civil War by the Soviet post-purge armed forces leadership created a hiatus to the development of theory and force structure for large-scale offensive and defensive operations. Only after bitter disappointments in its war against Finland and after observing the successes of the Germans against Poland and France did the Soviet High Command turn to the practical re-equipping and retraining of the armed forces for large-scale, mobile offensive and defensive operations. Unfortunately for the Soviets, their concepts of the strategic defensive had not been carefully thought out.[11]

The timing of Barbarossa acted like compound interest to Soviet failures, adding the incorrect anticipation of German operational methods. According to Maj. Gen. V. Matsulenko, despite reliable intelligence on German pre-attack troop concentrations, Soviet forces in the western military districts were not brought into proper combat readiness.[12] For instance, most of the first echelon divisions of Soviet covering force armies at the outbreak of war were located in training camps 8 to 20 kilometers from planned deployment lines. Additionally, comparatively few units were positioned directly adjacent to the frontier. Artillery and engineer units and signals subunits in certain armies were undergoing combat training in centers away from their parent formations; meanwhile, the covering forces armies' second echelons—usually mechanized corps—were 50 to 100 kilometers from the border and the district second echelon and reserve forces were as far away as 400 kilometers.[13] Not all of this can be explained by Stalin's willful neglect of political and strategic warnings of Hitler's hostile intentions, warnings received from numerous foreign and some domestic sources.[14] Some of the lack of prepared-ness in the border districts was because of changed borders, which occurred following the German–Soviet Pact of 1939. Pushing the bor-ders westward extended Soviet defensive lines over a broader front and required greater echeloning in depth for defense against a *blitz-krieg*. Rear logistics support, aircraft survivability, and command and control (for which the Soviet forces were inadequately trained and equipped by June 1941) were mistakenly thought to be replacing the need for traditional preparedness.

Lack of combat readiness in the western border military dis-tricts forced the Soviet leadership into operations to restore the dis-rupted strategic defensive front during the first weeks of war. The dilemmas presented to Soviet commanders were not unlike those that might recur in a modern version of Barbarossa with diminished post–Cold War Russian forces (at least, from the Russian military perspective). Restoration of a disrupted strategic front required that the Soviet leadership rethink political and military command and control arrangements. For strategic leadership of the war on June 23, 1941, the Main Command Headquarters (*STAVKA Glavnogo Komandovaniya*) was created, consisting of S. K. Timoshenko (chair-man); K. Ye Voroshilov; V. M. Molotov; I. V. Stalin; G. K. Zhukov; S. M. Budenny, and N. G. Kuznetsov. The Main Command Headquarters was subsequently transformed on July 10 into the Supreme Com-mand Headquarters (*Stavky Verkhovnogo Komandovaniya*) headed by Stalin and B. M. Shaposhnikov. On August 8, Stalin was named supreme commander in chief, and the headquarters was retitled Headquarters, Supreme High Command (*STAVKA, Verkhnogo Glamokomandovaniya* or STAVKA VGK).[15] To ensure unity of politi-cal and military command, STAVKA VGK carried out activities under the direction of the Party (VKP b, for "All-Union Communist Party, Bolshevik") Central Committee and Politburo, and according to guid-ance laid down by the State Committee for Defense (GKO, also headed by Stalin). The forces available to this command system in June 1941 are summarized in Table 1.

The most important measures to repel the German aggression and to restore the broken strategic defensive front were discussed at joint sessions of members of the Politburo, GKO, and STAVKA VGK.[16] To improve the command and control effectiveness and to facilitate military leadership of the fronts by the Supreme High Command, the State Defense Committee approved the creation of three intermedi-ate command and control organs on July 10. These were termed Main Commands of Troop Directions (Axes), or *glavniye komando-vaniya voysk napravleniya,* and were established as northwestern,

Table 1: Soviet Force Structure, June 1941

20 Armies
including: 6 in Far East, 3 partial

62 Rifle Corps
179 Rifle Divisions
19 Mountain Divisions
29 Mechanized Corps
61 Tank Divisions (58 in Mechanized Corps)
29 Motorized Divisions (in Mechanized Corps)
2 Motorized Rifle Divisions
4 Cavalry Corps
13 Cavalry Divisions (3 Mountain Cavalry)
5 Airborne Corps
15 Airborne Brigades (in Airborne Corps)
76 Artillery Regiments (howitzers and guns)
15 separate High Power Artillery Battalions
11 Mortar Battalions
10 Antitank Brigades
20 Antitank Regiments (in Antitank Brigades)

Overall Strength

Operating Forces – 4,900,000 men (2,900,000 in Western
     Military Districts)
Mobilized Force – 9,000,000 men

Source: David M. Glantz, "The Red Army in 1941," 1–37, in Glantz, ed., The
Initial Period of War on the Eastern Front, 22 June – August 1941 *(London: Frank
Cass, 1993), 28.*

western, and southwestern directions headed respectively by Marshal of the Soviet Union (MSU) K. Voroshilov, northwestern; MSU S.
K. Timoshenko (from July 19 MSU Shaposhnikov, and from July 30 Lt.
Gen. V. D. Sokolovskiy), western; and MSU S. M. Budenny (from September 1941 by Timoshenko), southwestern.[17]

These timely adjustments helped the Soviet armed forces to
stabilize and to reestablish the strategic defensive across several
fronts during the summer and autumn of 1941. Creating large defensive groups of forces that had not existed prior to war was accomplished by reassembling forces within fronts, by transferring units
from one front to another, and by moving strategic reserves from the

interior of the USSR.[18] Of course, this was difficult during the initial weeks of war, when German command of the air disrupted lines of communication and support, and forced Soviet units into battle under badly deployed and otherwise unfavorable conditions.

Even later Soviet forces were not always prepared for a rapid shift from offensive to defensive operations. For example, when the German Army Group Center aimed at the Smolensk–Moscow axis shifted to the offensive for its final lunge at Moscow in late September, it caught many of the defenders unprepared. A headquarters directive to Soviet forces on September 27 to halt their offensives in that sector and to shift to defensive operations caught most commanders with insufficient time to prepare terrain, complete engineering work, and reorganize formations for defensive battle.[19] Therefore, the Germans broke through the strategic defensive front and created a critical situation for the defense of Moscow. The Soviet High Command was forced to transfer units quickly from the northwestern and southwestern areas and to commit new strategic reserves against the thrusts of Army Group Center.[20] Within approximately one week, the Soviets organized what amounted to a new defensive configuration on the Moscow direction, contributing to the stalled German offensive on the Moscow axis in October. This success also allowed time for establishing a more favorable strategic defense of the Moscow direction by early November, including the forces of several fronts and of the Moscow Defense Zone that halted the German offensive at the gates of Moscow.[21]

A command and control challenge of equal seriousness confronted the Soviet High Command as early as June 1941 when it faced the need to conduct a general withdrawal of the decimated forces on the western strategic direction. It was clear to the Soviet leadership by June 25 that the main thrust of the German offensive was not against the southwestern direction (Kiev), as prewar planners under the influence of Stalin had assumed, but on the western direction along the line of Minsk–Smolensk–Moscow. Once this situation was clear, STAVKA VGK moved forces of seven armies to restore the disrupted front and to reinforce the forces defending the Moscow axis. Between June 27 and July 10, the Soviets transferred five combined arms armies (some thirty-six divisions) to the Western Front. An additional thirteen combined arms armies (104 divisions and thirty-three brigades) were eventually sent to reinforce the defense of the Moscow axis against the onslaught of Army Group Center.[22] Soviet defenders built defensive structures and engineer obstacles at rapid rates, and together with the reinforcement of reserves from the Supreme High Command and the transfer of forces from other fronts, they succeeded in a stubborn resistance against enemy attackers and caused delay and attrition sufficient to force German Army Group Center onto the temporary defensive by the end of July.[23]

If the Soviet command system provided for some necessary adaptations to the strategic defensive, it has nevertheless been held accountable for numerous shortcomings in the command and control of troops by Soviet military historians. For example, Lt. Gen. P. V. Maltsev in October 1988 wrote an article in the *Military-Historical Journal* titled "Who Is to Blame?"[24] Maltsev was commander of a machine-gun platoon in the 111th Rifle Division on the Northwestern Front in June 1941. His article points to a number of shortcomings in the command and control arrangements for the defense of the Western Special Military District (later the Western Front).

Staffs were, according to Maltsev's account, deficient in numbers of personnel and in communications equipment. Even the district signals troops lacked regulation communications equipment. Communications with troops were based on permanent telephone and telegraph lines of the USSR People's Commissariat of Communications. This state wire network was organized under a radial plan in which communications centers and lines were concentrated in large industrial and administrative centers. Thus, overhead communications lines along major rail and road arteries and communication centers in heavily populated areas were vulnerable to air interdiction and other attacks.[25] Radio communications were inadequate for combat tasks: radio operators in the district forces were insufficiently trained. Military councils of the district and its armies had no concept of the speed with which a surprise attack could inflict devastating losses on them; additionally, they lacked skills in organizing and maintaining cooperation between various branches of troops and were restricted by lack of initiative. Front command was prohibited by order of the People's Commissar of Defense from provocative actions, the term "provocative" being defined to include what most other armies fighting on the defensive would consider reasonable measures for self-defense.

Disruption of communications by enemy sabotage groups added to the confusion created by the complexity of code tables. Commanders often issued orders in clear that were intercepted by the enemy, and many communications came too late for most formations to take up their required defensive positions on time.[26] The front commander issued combat orders, one after another, which failed to take into account the actual situation; staff of the front did not know whether orders were actually reaching the troops.[27] According to Maltsev, loss of control over the troops and ignorance of the true state of affairs on the part of district commanders (who in turn were cut off from the Supreme High Command for a considerable period) led to decisions that were "unrealistic and infeasible," as well as to the "absence of control over the execution of issued orders."[28] This experience is not confined to history. It has been repeated as recently as 1991, when Russians fought Iraqis with Soviet equipment and using Soviet air defense and command-control tactics. In contrast, the U.S. air war effectively decapitated the Iraqi air defense network and military command-control system in about a week of round-the-clock air sorties.

Writing in the *Military-Historical Journal* in November 1988, Maj. Gen. Kunitskiy asked how the Soviet armed forces were able to carry out a successful winter offensive in 1941–1942 to push the enemy back from Moscow.[29] Yet, by mid July 1942, the strategic initiative was again in enemy hands: German troops had broken Soviet strategic defenses for the fourth time and placed the armed forces of the USSR in extreme jeopardy in the southwest, the direction of Stalingrad and the Northern Caucasus. (Three breakthroughs had occurred during offensives of the previous year's campaigns.) The standard explanation for the ability of the Germans to regain the initiative in 1942, according to Kunitskiy, had been German superiority in forces. He rejects that explanation and presents statistics to demonstrate that in crucial levels of manpower and equipment, Soviet forces were not inferior to the German.[30] The Wehrmacht breached the Soviet defensive front once again, he argues, because of miscalculation by STAVKA VGK in planning the 1942 summer campaigns. The Supreme High Command overestimated the capabilities of the Soviet armed forces relative to the German forces on the basis of the successful offensives conducted by the Red Army during the previous winter. The Soviet General Staff had offered more pessimistic assessments of Soviet capabilities, but they were not heeded.[31]

According to Kunitskiy, STAVKA VGK also wrongly predicted the direction of the main thrust of German forces. Soviet military intelligence reported to the General Staff on March 18, 1942, that German troop preparations indicated a spring offensive centered on the southern sector toward Stalingrad and the Northern Caucasus. STAVKA VGK judged instead that the Germans would launch their main thrust on the flank of Soviet Army Central Grouping with the objectives of Moscow and the central industrial region of the USSR.[32] This mistake was not corrected until the pressure created by the German offensives forced rethinking at the end of June, when the Soviet High Command began reorganizing the defensive fronts in the region. On July 12, the new Stalingrad Front was established, including three reserve armies from STAVKA VGK.[33] On the Northern Caucasus sector, the Southern and Northern Caucasus fronts were combined into a single Northern Caucasus Front on July 28. To ensure effective command and control on the Stalingrad sector, STAVKA VGK decided on August 5 to split the Stalingrad Front into the independent Stalingrad Front (commanded by Lt. Gen.V. N. Gordov) and the Southeastern Front (commanded by Col. Gen. A. I. Yeremenko). For operational purposes the Stalingrad Front was ordered to cover the city from the west and northwest and to defeat the enemy that had broken through the inner defensive perimeter at the boundary of the 21st and 62nd armies. The Southeastern Front was to stop the German advance toward the southern face of the outer defense perimeter and to prevent the Wehrmacht in that sector from reaching the Volga to the south of Stalingrad.[34]

Soviet preparedness for war indicated how well the General Staff of the Soviet armed forces understood the operational doctrines of potential opponents.[35] Intelligence was expected to convey adequate "order of battle" data as well as hostile intent. It must also establish how the opponent was going to fight if combat occurred. As Richard K. Betts and other experts on intelligence have pointed out, there is a great deal of difference between adequacy of warning and effectiveness of response.[36] In between warning and response is the psychologically based but intelligence-driven "threat perception," which is highly subjective. Part of this threat perception is the military operational doctrine according to which war plans will be implemented. For example, potential defenders need to know whether the opponent's strategy is one of blitzkrieg or of a slow war of attrition.[37] Or, in nuclear strategy, regardless of whether the actual outcome of such a war is judged to be "winnable" by either side, it matters whether selective and limited attacks are planned in the initial phases of a superpower conflict. For example, deterrence may be affected by American or Soviet leaders' expectations about how the other will respond to limited attacks by selective rather than general retaliation.[38]

As Michael I. Handel has noted, a critical issue for students of surprise attack is the time lag between the adequacy of attacker preparations for surprise assault and defender preparations to meet the attack. The difference between attacker and defender preparedness for war is more complicated than the comparatively simpler issue of warning time. Warning may be given but response, in the form of timely mobilization by the defender, may be delayed or postponed entirely.[39] Since surprise is rarely complete and total, defenders have usually begun some mobilization and response. The more precise questions then become how much mobilization and how timely? Handel refers to the time between the victim's (of surprise) preparations for war and the attacker's imminent actions as the "readiness gap." The ratio between the readiness gap and the defender's actual mobilization is therefore a valid conceptual indicator of the effectiveness of a surprise attack, with two exceptions.[40] First, a defender could have obtained irrefutable information of a forthcoming attack and have decided to preempt, although its forces have not yet been fully mobilized. An example of this might be the Israeli attack on Egypt in 1967. Second, one side could have won the race to mobilize fully but delayed its attack, allowing the opponent time and opportunity to improve its own preparations. This exception has at times occurred during an extended crisis, for example, during the July crisis of 1914.[41]

Col. Gen. M. A. Gareev, deputy chief of the Soviet General Staff, wrote in 1985 that Soviet military theory and operational plans on the eve of World War II gave insufficient attention to the proper conduct of the operational and strategic defensive. He noted that the

> idea of the continuous shifting of war at its very outset to enemy territory (and the idea was unsound both scientifically and backed up neither by an analysis of the actual situation or by operational calculations) had so beguiled certain leading military workers that the possibility of conducting military operations on our own territory was virtually excluded.[42]

This same assessment is offered by Andrei Kokoshin and Valentin Larionov in their discussion of the Battle of Kursk as a model for the implementation of the doctrine of defensive sufficiency.[43] The authors do not dwell on the fact that Kursk was an example of very active defense nor that it was based on acquiring precise intelligence about the opponent's intentions. Kursk was also a case of an operational counteroffensive planned and conducted after war had been declared and fought for several years. Thus it provided little in the way of guidance for harried Soviet planners who might be tasked to defend expansive borders by force posture and military doctrine without preemption or active defense as options. As will be discussed further, Kokoshin and Larionov outlined four versions of possible defensive military doctrines that could serve the Soviet Union or others under modern conditions.

The Soviet experience with Barbarossa teaches two lessons that have the potential to create significant trade-offs in commitments of

intelligence and planning assets. The first lesson, openly acknowledged by Soviet commentators for many years, is that large-scale
operational defeats can be inflicted if sufficient forces and means are
planned ahead and the attacker successfully executes a deception
plan. The second lesson is that operational surprise, even on a large
scale, does not necessarily equate strategic victory. Soviet experience with Hitler's surprise offensive taught that attackers who base
operative constructs on victory in the initial period can overreach if
war becomes protracted. Some Soviet military theorists of the 1920s
and 1930s expressed skepticism that wars could be won in their initial period against territorially large and well-armed defenders. Their
assertion was confirmed during World War II when Hitler's blitzkrieg
defeated the Poles and French but not the Soviet Union. The French,
however, can be classified as equal adversaries of Hitler, although
Poland was outmatched against the Wehrmacht (and politically scis-
sored by the Nazi–Soviet nonaggression pact). Therefore, under the
right conditions, surprise, combined with effective weight of blow,
can prove strategically, operationally, and tactically decisive.[44]

In summary, the initial period of war on the Eastern Front was
nothing less than an imposed military transformation of the Soviet
armed forces. The Wehrmacht ran riot over its Soviet military opponent during the summer and fall of 1941, inflicting nearly catastrophic
losses and demonstrating that the Soviet prewar military was a "colossus with feet of clay."[45] The STAVKA and the General Staff were
forced to rebuild an entirely new army capable of conducting mobile
offensive and defensive operations on a large scale under the conditions of modern war.

Despite some important setbacks, by mid-1943 efforts to reconstitute a new army had been accomplished with the nucleus of large
tank and mechanized forces supported by modernized and better
equipped air, artillery, and engineering forces.[46] What this means for
the Russian army of the twenty-first century is that, unlike its Soviet predecessor, Russians will not have years to reconstitute themselves if the armed forces are subjected to the degree of surprise at
the outset of war that befell Stalin on June 22, 1941.

Surprise and Deception: Lessons from Manchuria

Russian military thinking is greatly concerned with the problem of
surprise. Soviet military doctrine placed surprise among the most
important principles of military art. An important component of surprise was deception, or *maskirovka*. Maskirovka is an inclusive concept in Soviet and Russian military thought. According to Col. David
M. Glantz, who studied extensively Soviet use of deception in World

War II, Soviet military theorists contended that surprise could be achieved by one or more of the following methods:

- misleading the enemy with regard to one's intentions
- maintaining the secrecy of one's plans
- concealing combat preparations
- using new weapons, techniques, and forms of combat
- choosing correctly the direction of the main blow and correctly timing its delivery
- Using all types of forces, especially air, artillery, and armored forces in surprise attacks
- maneuvering rapidly and acting decisively to forestall enemy responses
- using fraudulent structures, communications, or other means for deception (e.g., dummy weapons, false communications)
- using effectively the terrain, weather, and seasonal factors.[47]

According to Glantz, maskirovka applies directly to five of these nine conditions and indirectly affects them all. One implication for contemporary Russian planners is that the command and control of friendly forces, including the initial organization, must be concealed to the full extent possible. Demonstrations, simulations, and diversionary attacks can confuse enemy intelligence about the choice of primary attack sector. Disinformation (*dezinformatsiya*) exploits enemy perceptions of one's own capabilities and intentions.[48] The Russians have demonstrated agility in the art of deception and disinformation and will attempt to exploit this agility for gains immediately prior to war, during the initial period of war, and throughout the duration of a conflict.

The nature of deception before and during the initial period becomes even more important with the threat of nuclear weapons facing potential Russian defenders or attackers. Disinformation, in this context, could allow the Russian leadership to exploit opponents who lack internal consensus on goals or methods.[49]

In particular, Russian efforts in the initial period to deceive potential opponents could involve leading an enemy to believe, for example, that mobilizing Russia's military machine and economic base for war required an extensive period. Instead, measures would be implemented to prepare forces for war without depending on massive and highly visible general mobilization. Instead, new technical means would reinforce rapidly and secretly selected forward-deployed forces.

Russian mobilization without detection could also be accomplished by exploiting past Soviet experience and generating new units from existing "cadre" or skeletal units, which are kept on standby status with only portions of their necessary wartime equipment and personnel available in peacetime.[50] Wartime force strength and operational configuration may not be apparent from peacetime deployments and organization of the Russian armed forces, according to some expert western analysts. Peacetime force structure may perform administrative and maskirovka functions. Forces may be rearranged on a geographical or functional (operational configuration, or *operativnoye postroeniye*) basis during the period immediately prior to war or in the initial period itself. Glantz offers an example: before the dissolution of the Warsaw Pact, the 19th Division Group of Soviet Forces, Germany (GSFG), was expected by western intelligence to produce a single wartime front (roughly comparable to a NATO Army Group). In fact, with minimum reinforcement and resubordination of units on a more logical geographical or functional basis, GSFG could actually have formed two fronts, each having at least three armies.[51]

Military deceptions can be active or passive and directed at misleading the opponent regarding a state's capabilities or its intentions.[52] Many actions that western analysts classified as deception fell into distinct programs in Soviet intelligence policy and were, therefore, the responsibility of separate security organizations. These Soviet activities included maskirovka counterintelligence and active measures.[53] Maskirovka was the kind of deception of most direct applicability to Soviet military planning; it includes camouflage, cover, and denial of information to the opponent, as well as active and passive efforts at deception.[54] Maskirovka applied at the strategic, operational, and tactical levels of Soviet military planning; at all levels, it supported the secrecy of Soviet planning and operations and of disorienting the enemy as to Soviet intentions and capabilities.[55] As Michael Handel has noted, the success of deception operations, especially complicated ones, depends on the patient creation of misleading images and expectations in the minds of opponents. Thus, successful deception requires enough time for the various threads to be brought together by the enemy's own intelligence services. In addition, deception operations must be designed without redundant, self-defeating complexity. The deception requires that conclusions rise "naturally" in the course of the victim's intelligence collection and estimation.[56]

The importance of strategic and operational deception in wartime operations was demonstrated, according to Soviet military historians, by a successful strategic operation in the Far East in 1945 against the Japanese Kwantung Army. The Soviets overcame significant obstacles, including timely regroupment of forces; logistical support of forward, fast-moving tactical elements in battle; and command and control of a multifront operation. The operational triumph was partly dependent on deceiving the Japanese about exact timing and method of attack.[57] To accomplish their objective of defeating the Kwantung Army and preventing any of its elements from withdrawing outside of Manchuria, the Soviets were required to use the combined forces of three fronts on widely separated axes over a frontage of more than four thousand miles. The main thrust was launched by forces of the Transbaikal Front, which was required to move four all-arms armies and a tank army across the Great Khingan Mountains. Planning for the Manchurian offensive began in March 1945, and a major regroupment of forces from Europe to Asia took place from May through July.[58]

The massive regroupment of Soviet forces prior to launching the Manchurian operation also required a major change in previous wartime command and control practices, both of which were important to conceal from Japanese intelligence until the moment of attack. By 1944, Soviet experience in the Second World War had demonstrated the ability to conduct operations over several fronts and multiple axes of advance under the coordination of STAVKA representatives dispatched by Stalin to the various theaters of operation. Planning for the offensive against the Japanese in Manchuria soon revealed, however, that an innovative arrangement in the command system would be required for the Far Eastern theater. Thus, a Far Eastern theater headquarters was established under Marshal A. M. Vasilevskiy, who was responsible for all land, air, and sea operations in the Far East and Transbaikal regions.[59] The Far East High Command carried out a plan to defeat the Kwantung Army by a strategic "Cannae," or envelopment, using three fronts, each assigned a strategic axis of advance: Transbaikal Front on the Transbaikal–Manchurian axis, second Far Eastern Front on the Amur–Manchurian axis, and first Far Eastern Front on the Maritime–Manchurian axis. The forces of the Transbaikal Front were to advance rapidly against major Japanese defensive bastions—including Mukden—and eventually to link up with the forces of first Far Eastern Front to complete encirclement.

From the point of view of Soviet strategic and policy objectives, it was important not only to defeat the remnants of Kwantung Army in Manchuria but to do so quickly and decisively. Thus, deception planning needed to allow for the unprecedented regrouping and concentration of forces ("the largest regrouping of forces in history," according to S. P. Ivanov, who as chief of staff of the Soviet Far Eastern Command in August 1945, is understandably enthusiastic).[60] Nonetheless, it cannot be denied that movement of equipment and supplies from the European to the Far Eastern theater of operations covered a distance of nine thousand to twelve thousand miles over rail and road networks, which were far from optimal for the purpose. Redeployment of Soviet forces from Europe to Asia in several months doubled Soviet strength in the Far East from a previous forty divisions to more than eighty. David M. Glantz observes,

> The movement of men and material eastward involved constant use of screening, cover, and secrecy. The Soviets relied heavily on night movement to deceive the Japanese as to the grand scale of redeployment. Use of assembly areas remote from the border masked attack intentions, but ultimately required units to move to the attack in August over a considerable distance. Many high-ranking commanders moved into the theater under assumed names and wore the rank[s] of junior officers. While the sheer size of Soviet movements made them impossible to mask, deceptive measures obscured the scale of Soviet redeployments and caused the Japanese to underestimate the Soviet ability to attack.[61]

The Manchurian campaign is an important one for the present-day student of Russian military thinking. It showed how using the component of surprise decisively exploited and followed up contributes to a successful strategic offensive operation. S. P. Ivanov underscores this. The Far Eastern campaign against Japan, he declares, was "truly one of Blitzkrieg warfare," which had a "decisive influence" on the Japanese decision to end their participation in the Second World War (more decisive, according to Ivanov, than the United States dropping atomic bombs on Hiroshima and Nagasaki).[62] In addition, studying the Far East campaign can contribute a great deal toward forming the modern Soviet art of war. Ivanov states that one lesson is that surprise "was a decisive factor in achieving rapid success in the campaign," as was the ability of the Soviet High Command to keep secret the plans for the offensive, the time of launching the attack on Japanese forces, the main strategic directions of attack, and the composition of attacking Soviet forces.[63]

Perhaps a more profound lesson from the Manchurian campaign is that an essentially defensive or holding operation in a major theater of strategic military action may be turned rapidly into a launching pad for an offensive operation with a high probability of success. As studies by Handel and other experts on military surprise have shown, surprise does not need to be total to be strategic, in other words, to be politically or militarily decisive in its effects.[64] Historical cases of surprise also show that the weaker combatant can exploit the vulnerability of the stronger to overconfidence. Finally, the defender can surprise the attacker by moving more rapidly than thought possible from an essentially defensive posture to a potentially offensive one. Strategic nuclear weapons make this transition from defensive/nonthreatening to offensive/threatening postures possible within minutes, as is widely acknowledged. Less widely acknowledged is the possibility of doing the same over a longer period with conventional forces, especially with the advantages of historical experience and military art as incentives.

Russia, the Revolution in Military Affairs, and Future Security

Russian president Vladimir Putin moved quickly to improve relations with the United States in the aftermath of the terrorist attacks of 9/11. Russia offered its intelligence support for American military operations in Afghanistan against the Taliban and al Qaeda and raised no objection to U.S. military deployments in several former Soviet Central Asian states. President Putin sought to use improved security cooperation with the United States to expedite a *zapadpolitik*, or western policy, of greater economic and security cooperation with the European Union. This policy also promoted a higher profile for Russia in NATO's consultative machinery, although not a veto over NATO decisions. President Putin's western policy was controversial within Russian policymaking circles: some military elites distrusted the concept of a new security regime between Washington and Moscow. President Bush's decision to withdraw from the ABM Treaty, announced in December 2001, created additional skepticism among Russians opposed to further U.S.–Russian security cooperation, as did the beginning of U.S. national missile defense deployments in 2004. But President Putin and President Bush agreed to further reductions in offensive nuclear weapons under the Strategic Offensive Reductions Treaty (SORT) of May 2002.

Russian military planners in the early years of the twenty-first century, like their professional colleagues in other countries, are required to plan for possible as well as likely deployment scenarios. A net assessment of Russia's geostrategic position in the current international environment could not have been reassuring to its General Staff and main force commanders at the dawn of the present century. NATO anticipated and enlarged its membership. China engaged in a large-scale military buildup. India and Pakistan became acknowledged holders of nuclear bombs. The Bush administration followed its rapid campaign to oust the Taliban from power in Afghanistan in 2001 with its "shock and awe" machinations to depose Saddam Hussein and his regime in Iraq in 2003. In addition, U.S. military deployments for combat actions, combat service support, or military advice against terrorism were taking place in former Soviet Central Asia and the Caucasus.

Faced with this alignment of political and military forces, Russia maintained an underfunded and poorly trained military that was fully engaged in trying to suppress rebellion in the republic of Chechnya. President Putin was more resolute in opposing Chechnya's territorial independence to an extremity of destruction after 1999 than his predecessor, Boris Yeltsin, had been from 1994 to 1996. Russia's military performance in Chechnya after 1999 benefitted from its mistakes in the earlier war: the Russian General Staff committed many more troops with improved training and coordination among various arms of service. Nevertheless, Chechen resistance remained active through 2002, although it was mostly contained in redoubts in the southern and more mountainous portion of the rebellious province. Since it had no military clout to spare from its cash-starved conventional forces, Russia was forced to rely on its nuclear deterrent to cover threats of large-scale conventional war or military aggression against Russia or its neighboring states.

In addition to an expanding NATO, encirclement by troubled or ambitious regional partners, and a deficient conventional military establishment, early twenty-first-century Russia faced the inevitable need to adjust to postmodern warfare and the impact of advanced technology, conventional weapons, and command-control systems. Even if Russia could rebuild the Soviet Union's ground forces of the 1980s it would not suffice to ensure against future threats based on newer weapons and the strategies made possible by post-industrial technology. Post-industrial or third-wave warfare created a new military cyberspace in which the capability for systems integration across the parts of a knowledge-based strategy would prove to be decisive. The various parts included command, control, communications, and computers (C4); intelligence, surveillance, and reconnaissance (ISR); long-range, precision strike; and stealth technology. Even if Russia had the military-industrial complex that it had during the Soviet era, it would still lag in smart technology on account of its underdeveloped private sector economy. Russian economic performance improved in 2000 and 2001 relative to 1999, mostly because of oil prices but also on account of a widespread perception of stronger state leadership.

Improved economic performance is a necessary, but not a sufficient, condition for a Russian army that can cope with third-wave, post-industrial warfare. Smart soldiers and innovative commanders who can think "out of the box" are as important as technology as the nature of warfare shifts from massive battles of attrition to flexible and small-scale military operations. In addition, future warfare will take place in at least five dimensions: land, sea, air, space, and cyberspace. These multiple environments for future war fighting make the challenges posed by the "initial period of war" especially problematical for technically backward militaries. The possibility of strategic losses within minutes or seconds in the opening phase of war, including a possible cyberwar that would create chaos with exclusively electronic casualties, is now within the reach of feasible or foreseeable military art.

Russia's national security concept of the year 2000 and its related military doctrine show its fears of surprise attack in the face of NATO conventional military superiority. This concern became especially acute in the period immediately following NATO's 1999 war against Yugoslavia, coincident with the official enlargement of NATO to include Poland, Hungary, and the Czech Republic. NATO's Operation Allied Force forced a historic Russian ally to capitulate to the alliance's demands for repatriation of Albanian Kosovars by means of an air war alone, without resorting to ground invasion. Russia rushed in at the endgame to make a dramatic gesture of deploying its share of the peacekeeping force into Kosovo. But NATO's willingness to go to war for the first time in its history and in the face of Russian objections, bypassing the UN Security Council, advertised Russia's post–Cold War military backwardness in technologies related to the Revolution in Military Affairs. Russia's draft military doctrine of 1999 and its national security concept of 2000 therefore opened the door to the possible use of nuclear weapons not only for deterrence but also for war fighting. The security concept stated that Russia's use of nuclear weapons would become possible "in the event or need to repulse armed aggression, if all other measures of resolving the crisis situation have been exhausted and proven ineffective."[65]

The estimation of the wartime environment from the peacetime one was difficult enough before the age of automation and "electronization." In the future, additional complexity will be added to efforts to extrapolate from peacetime to wartime by the higher degree of uncertainty about wartime command and control and by the higher degree of interdependency among command, communications, control, and intelligence functions. This suggests three immediate implications for Russian military planners. First, the battle for control over the electromagnetic spectrum will become more intense in the future, compared with the past: electronic countermeasures and counter-countermeasures (ECM and ECCM, respectively) will figure more prominently in procurement and exercises for all modern armies, navies, and air forces.

Second, the pressure to acquire additional combat power from a reduced or restructured force—albeit one postured defensively—means that command must be pushed downward as far as possible. Tactical flexibility will be a necessary condition to accomplish battlefield objectives that would otherwise remain at risk. Soviet operations in the Great Patriotic War were designed for a command and control system that maximized operational and strategic commander's flexibility at the expense of severely restrictive guidelines for tactical commanders (in the Soviet ground forces, division or lower).[66]

Third, offensive and defensive information warfare, including both information-supported military operations and information-based psychological warfare against enemy societies gains a new priority status as a topic for the armed forces general staff. Russia has now seen the United States fight four wars or multinational peace operations based more or less on information superiority: Operation Desert Storm in 1991, Kosovo in 1999, Afghanistan in 2001, and Iraq in 2003.[67]

Defensive military doctrine and electronization of the battlefield will create stronger pressures for the decentralization of decision-making authority, along with more widely distributed information technology needed by commanders to perform traditional tasks faster. Although armed forces are frequently studied from the perspectives of their military doctrine or combat tactics, they are less frequently analyzed as holistic institutions subject to periods of institutional steadiness or stress. Institutions are norm driven organizations that attempt to adapt to the unexpected by retracing their steps through familiar repertoires of memory, information, and procedure.[68] Beyond a certain point, incremental adaptation to a radically different environment is no longer possible: the organization must change its institutional ethos or cease to function with the same set of role perceptions. It can continue as an organization but not as the same institution it once was. One can apply this analysis to the changes now buffeting the Russian military as it attempts to transition from a mostly conscript to a contract service force and from the Soviet inheritance of a manpower-intensive force to a postmodern force capable of exploiting advanced technology for rapid reaction and contingency operations. In the judgment of some leading post-Soviet

Russian commanders, Russia had no option but to adapt to this information-based military template:

> The massive use of aviation and long-range precision weap-
> ons; electronic countermeasures; and integrated use of
> space information assets—all these approaches have be-
> come a firm part of U.S. military threats beginning with
> Operation Desert Storm against Iraq in 1991. Moreover,
> the primary targets in the course of the conflict were
> clearly specified: key installations of the economic infra-
> structure, elements of the state and military command
> and control system, and lines of transportation. NATO's
> eastward enlargement not only radically altered the force
> ratio in theatres of military operations but also permitted
> a number of kinds of tactical and operational-tactical
> weapons to perform strategic missions previously set aside
> for Pershing II missile complexes and cruise missiles.[69]

A microelectronic revolution in military affairs, following the
macroelectronic one, has recently begun to be appreciated by Russian military planners. Appropriate portable and desktop worksta-
tions as well as information bases diffused throughout the Russian
armed forces chain of command affect everything that armed forces
do. Further, a "smarter" Russian command and control system becomes a potential liability or a possible asset. Communications and
electronics technology can be effective in combat planning yet at
the same time creates vulnerability through dependence on the technology. Rising vulnerability correlates directly with the growth of
dependence. A particular danger for the Russian armed forces would
be having tactical units isolated and cut off from each other. Such an
outcome is not inconceivable to Soviet military planners; it happened in the week following June 22, 1941.[70]
    Another aspect of the electronic and automated battlefield was
demonstrated through the U.S. war in Afghanistan in 2001. It showed
that highly integrated intelligence, surveillance, and reconnaissance
systems, combined with long-range precision strike and advanced
control systems, can support the innovative use of operations and
tactics to overpower an adversary in the initial period of war.[71] Los-
ing command, control, and communications can affect combat stability and consequently the ability to fight a war with small unit
cohesion and combat system interdependence. If, for example, a
tactical air or air defense component of a modern ground force can
be electronically isolated from the remainder of the force, then the

remnants of that force can be swallowed up at the discretion of the opponent. Future war winning strategies below the threshold of nuclear escalation may rely on the "implosion" of the opponent's command and control system and the subsequent collapse of the opponent's ability to coordinate its various formations.

Conclusions

Russian and Soviet historical experience dictates that Russian military planners now need to assume great danger in the initial period of war. From the perspective of these risk-averse planners, Russian forces drawn back to the western border districts of the current federation will face an onslaught similar to that of Barbarossa in 1941. Russian intelligence will place equally high importance on detecting an enemy's strategic warning as on acquiring order of battle data and other information essential for response to tactical warning. Therefore, NATO would be well advised to continue its program of political and military collaboration with Russia and to encourage improvements in Russia's early warning and control systems so that they are less susceptible to self-generated default. In addition, NATO enlargement should deemphasize the alliance's nuclear guaranty as a last resort. In this regard, the United States and the Russian Federation would also be well advised to continue pursuit of strategic nuclear arms reductions agreed to in the Moscow Treaty of May 24, 2002, and scheduled to enter into effect by December 31, 2012.

However, Russia's "Barbarossa complex" cannot be permitted to stand in the way of meaningful military reform that has already been postponed for too long since the end of the Cold War. NATO's expansion to the borders of Belarus and the Ukraine occurs within a political climate of cooperative security between America and Russia. Russia is threatened primarily not by NATO but by threats of regional wars, internal terrorism, and insurgent wars for which the General Staff and Ministry of Defense must develop contingency planning. Preparedness for these contingencies of limited and local wars, regular and irregular, will require a smaller, more professional, and more mobile military than post-Soviet Russia has yet fielded. As well, Russia's armed forces, together with the General Staff and Ministry of Defense, must be made accountable to its political leadership as an institutional (not a personal) matter. Otherwise, Russia's armed forces and military doctrine will be unable to meet security challenges of the twenty-first century. A repeat of strategic surprise under the new conditions could involve significant territorial losses to neighbors or large-scale civilian casualties from the deadly effects of terrorist strikes with weapons of mass destruction.

2

RUSSIA AND MILITARY TRANSFORMATION: PERSPECTIVES FROM THE FIRST NUCLEAR AGE

Military transformations are brought about by drastic changes in the technology for war, the organization of warfare, or the ways and means of making war (strategy, operational art, and tactics).[1] The arrival of atomic and then thermonuclear weapons posed a major threat to the Soviet Union's military strategy. The Red Army had pushed the German Wehrmacht from Stalingrad to Berlin to win back Russian territory and liberate Eastern Europe. The basis of Soviet World War II military strategy was simple, if enormously destructive —mass, metal, and mobilization of all societal assets behind a protracted war of attrition. Based on climactic battles fought over immense theaters of operation and against Hitler's best legions, the Soviets errantly believed they were the masters of modern warfare. The detonation at Alamogordo Bombing Range on July 16, 1945, and the advent of modern strategic airpower and missilery reversed that assumption.

Thereafter came the Soviet adjustment to a nuclear armed world. Between 1945 and 1989, nuclear weapons affected Soviet thinking and planning for fighting or deterring a world war. Additionally, nuclear weapons affected the Soviets' ideas about strategic defense and prevention or conduct of a conventional war in Europe. The combination of acknowledged nuclear stalemate and escalated conventional defenses made possible a variety of East–West arms limitation agreements that helped to bring the Cold War to an end.[2]

As did the Soviet military high command and political leadership from 1945 until 1991, so, too are Russia's power ministries adapting to a twenty-first century posing new technology challenges and a restructured international system. Russia's nuclear weapons, carried forward from the former Soviet superpower, are currently its singular claim to major power status. But these weapons are also problematical

for Russia. In the aftermath of 9/11 and U.S–Russian security cooperation against global terrorism, Russia seeks to secure its nuclear
facilities and materials against unauthorized leakage to terrorists or
criminals and to prevent accidental or inadvertent war prompted by
failed technology or procedures.

The Soviet View of Deterrence

In the West, and especially in the United States, the idea of "deterrence" as the object of military force found a receptive military-
strategic culture, more so than in Russia. Generally speaking, Soviet
thinking was less centered on the military balance per se than it was
conditioned by the idea of "correlation of forces" (*sootnoshenie sil*),
a more inclusive construct that took into account political, social,
economic, and moral-psychological factors of the competing systems.
In addition, the Soviet view of deterrence was less oriented to nuclear
weapons and nuclear war than America's. Soviet leaders were equally
as concerned with avoiding a conventional war in Europe on unfavorable terms, among other reasons, because such a conflict could
become nuclear. Furthermore, the Soviet political leadership inherited a "defense of Mother Russia" or "Barbarossa complex" from
Russia's history of invasions from Poles, Swedes, French, Germans,
and others who ravaged its extended and vulnerable borders. This
explains why, despite the primitiveness of available technology and
in the face of American arms control biases against defenses, Russians took antimissile defense of the homeland quite seriously.[3]

Joseph Stalin publicly deprecated the value of atomic weapons
as long as the United States maintained a nuclear monopoly: pri-
vately, he urged on his own scientists and feared U.S. nuclear intimidation.[4] As Soviet military thinkers adapted to the availability of
plentiful nuclear weapons and long-range delivery systems, they developed concepts of deterrence and of crisis management considerably different from those familiar to Americans. The facts of Russian
and Soviet historical experience, the role of the professional armed
forces in setting down the "military science" aspects of military doctrine, and the geopolitical setting for Soviet postwar foreign policymaking all implied a uniquely Russian context for thinking about the
role of nuclear forces and of nuclear dissuasion in defense policy.[5]

Stalin's successors in the party leadership and their military
advisors acknowledged after 1953 that nuclear weapons had brought
about a revolution in military affairs. This acknowledgment came in
stages and arrived in full force only after Nikita Khrushchev disposed
of serious rivals for the party leadership in 1957. Between the time
of Stalin's death and his assumption of undisputed power in Moscow,

Khrushchev played a clever game against his most important rivals for leadership in the party and government: Georgiy Malenkov and Vyacheslav Molotov. In March 1954, Malenkov, then-chairman of the Council of Ministers of the USSR, asserted that any war between the United States and the Soviet Union "considering the modern means of warfare, would mean the end of civilization."[6] Malenkov's initiative had been prompted in part by a classified report prepared the same month by four prominent physicists associated with the Soviet nuclear weapons program. The scientists noted that within a few years, the stockpiles of atomic explosives would be sufficient to "create conditions under which the existence of life over the whole globe will be impossible" and added that "we cannot but admit that mankind faces an enormous threat of the termination of all life on Earth."[7]

Malenkov's expression of pessimism about the outcome of modern war was in contradiction to then-prevalent party and ideological orthodoxy. Khrushchev used Malenkov's alleged heresy to remove him from his leadership posts. Khrushchev then turned against Molotov, pushing him out of the foreign ministry and into eventual political obscurity. One of Khrushchev's arguments against Molotov was the latter's obduracy when confronted with the new political reality created by nuclear weapons. In 1956, the Twentieth Party Congress of the CPSU rejected the inevitability of world war between capitalism and socialism. Instead, party doctrine (as guided by Khrushchev) endorsed the thesis of "peaceful coexistence" between different social systems.[8]

Having deposed his principal rivals from the early post-Stalin years and having survived a later attempt to oust him from power by the "antiparty group," Khrushchev vacillated again on the question of nuclear weapons and military strategy. In the latter 1950s, he fully embraced the idea of nuclear missile warfare as the centerpiece of Soviet military planning guidance.[9] He was left with the problem of explaining how socialism would survive and triumph in the aftermath of a global nuclear war with the Americans and their NATO allies. After Khrushchev's departure from the top posts in party and government in 1964, party guidance continued to insist that socialism would prevail even in nuclear war.[10] However, under Leonid Brezhnev and his successors, military doctrine was adjusted to allow the problem of nuclear escalation to be considered as a variable instead of a constant.

Soviet military literature in the early 1960s emphasized that war would probably begin with a massive nuclear surprise attack and involve the Soviet Union and its allies against the West in a major coalition war. The military thinking that appeared in these studies was no mere theoretical exercise. War plans of the early 1960s made similar assumptions about nuclear missile use within the European theater of military actions and between the American and Soviet homelands. For example, the 1964 Warsaw Pact plan for war in Europe, prepared and approved by the Soviet General Staff, discounted NATO's declared strategy of fighting a defensive war on its own soil as a hoax. Instead, Soviet commanders were told to anticipate that NATO would follow an offensive war plan, including early nuclear fire strikes against vital targets in Eastern Europe and in the Soviet Union.[11] To fight and prevail under the extreme conditions of a war including nuclear weapons, Soviet political leaders would need to anticipate the outbreak of a war and to authorize military commanders to engage in prompt offensives that employed theater and, if necessary, strategic nuclear weapons. As Vojtech Mastny explained,

> The Soviet generals, however, were no fools. They knew well enough that NATO was preparing for a defense against them. But they were so mesmerized by their still vivid memories of the very nearly successful German surprise attack on their country in 1941 that they could not imagine any other reliable strategy than that of striking at the enemy before he could strike at them.[12]

If Soviet generals were no fools, neither were their atomic scientists and more astute field commanders. It might be an article of faith for the High Command, reflecting Communist Party oversight, that nuclear combat in Europe or globally could be sustained at a high intensity and to an acceptable outcome. But it was apparent that even in a "limited" nuclear war the amount of destruction that would take place in a short time would be unprecedented and complicate military offensive and defensive operations planning. An authoritative account of current military doctrine was prepared in August 1964 by then-chief of Soviet military intelligence, Col. Gen. P. Ivashutin, for the head of the Military Academy of the General Staff. The account relates the struggle to reconcile the political imperative for victory in combat with the nontraditional reality of nuclear weapons:

> As a result of the mutual exchanges of nuclear strikes, an exceptionally difficult situation would emerge in the theater of military action. Numerous fires, destruction, flooding, and high radiation levels will most likely slow or completely stop any kind of movement of the troops that survived

nuclear strikes on a number of directions, especially immediately after the nuclear strikes. However, one would
suppose that the situation would not be the same everywhere. . . . It is quite probable that there would be a sufficient number of directions in the theater where the troops,
which preserved their combat capability, could conduct
forward operations at least some time after the nuclear
strikes, and we should be able to use such directions.[13]

One possible way to reconcile nontraditional technology with
traditional objectives in war was to develop and deploy missile defenses. Soviet interest in missile defense in the latter 1950s and
early 1960s cut across arms of service and politico-military factions
within the party and armed forces leadership. So-called radicals, who
subscribed enthusiastically to Khrushchev's view of future war as
dominated by nuclear missile weapons, were interested in missile
defenses as potential offsets to the enemy's main weapons of attack.
On the other side, "conservatives" feared the possibility of protracted
war involving both nuclear and conventional military forces and
emphasized the importance of defenses in protecting the Soviet
economy and industry. All three editions of the authoritative *Military Strategy* (1962, 1963, and 1968) offered some support for the
role of missile defense systems in Soviet military strategy, although
with some ambivalence as to the quality of BMD technology.[14]

Following Khrushchev's ouster in 1964 and changes in U.S. and
allied NATO strategy toward "flexible response" in the second half of
the 1960s, Soviet military strategists showed increased interest in
scenarios other than massive retaliation and global conflict.[15] As
the decade progressed a variety of authoritative political and military thinkers acknowledged that large-scale war could be waged with
conventional weapons only. In addition, the potential payoff from
Soviet support for wars of "national liberation" against pro-western
states outside of Europe directed additional military thinking toward
local and limited wars. Soviet military thinking in the 1950s and
1960s can be summarized as

- a massive nuclear but relatively short war in which strategic nuclear weapons played the major role in deciding the
  outcome
- a more protracted war including nuclear strikes but also
  involving all of the armed forces
- a major war in which nuclear weapons are used in a restricted
  or limited manner in one or several theaters of military action

- a major war limited to the use of conventional weapons
- a local war involving conventional weapons.[16]

The willingness of Soviet military analysts to entertain multiple scenarios as equally valid possibilities increased in the 1970s as a result of detente between the United States and the Soviet Union. New threat assessments were also mandated by the geopolitical repositioning of China, henceforth treated as an ally of the United States and NATO.[17]

The period of threat preceding war—as explained by lecturers at the Soviet General Staff Academy during the 1970s—was a time in which the Soviet armed forces were in great danger of being caught by surprise.[18] In a nuclear war the ability to seize the strategic initiative in the first minutes would have, according to these estimates, a decisive impact on military action and the duration and outcome of the conflict. Soviet forces must be prepared for transition from conventional to nuclear operations at any moment. The first volume of the lecture materials from the General Staff Academy discussed the "forms of initiation of war by the aggressor" and, with regard to NATO, specified the possibilities as

- surprise strikes with unlimited use of nuclear weapons
- a strike with initially limited use of nuclear weapons and subsequently converting to full use of the complete nuclear arsenal
- strikes by groupings of armed forces deployed in the TSMAs (TVDs) without the use of nuclear weapons
- initiation of war by gradual expansion of local wars.[19]

Initiation of war by the United States and its NATO allies through a general nuclear attack was studied in the 1970s as "the basic form of initiating war, with respect to American doctrine"[20] and was considered the most dangerous with the greatest consequences if unexpected and not reacted to promptly. The Soviet lecturers described at some length how the United States would have orchestrated a nuclear surprise attack.[21] Although the most dangerous from the Soviet standpoint, this course of action *was not* judged to be the most likely, according to the Voroshilov lecture materials. More likely was the limited use of nuclear weapons, followed by the unlimited use of the U.S. and NATO complete arsenals.[22]

On the threshold of nuclear first use, knowing when NATO decided on nuclear escalation was of vital importance for Soviet intelligence. Subsequent reactive movements of troops, command posts, logistics, and other assets and the preparation of counterstrikes would have to take place during the time between detection of NATO's decision to go nuclear and the launching of the first salvos. Otherwise the Soviet and allied forces thrusting into central Europe would be confronted with a Barbarossa on the move, leading to a disruption of their attack plans, tempo of operations, and combat stability.

Soviet sensitivity to these possibilities was apparently acute in the early 1980s. During NATO command post exercise "Able Archer" conducted in November 1983, Warsaw Pact intelligence monitored the flow of events according to tasking laid down by experience and precedent. The exercise included practice with NATO nuclear release procedures.[23] British and American listening posts detected unusual Soviet sensitivity to unfolding events, with a significant increase in the volume and sense of urgency in Warsaw Pact message traffic.[24] On November 8–9, according to Soviet defector Oleg Gordievsky, an Operation Ryan message was sent from Moscow Center to KGB residencies abroad. Operation Ryan (for *raketno yadernoye napadeniye*, or "rocket nuclear attack") had been established in 1981 for intelligence gathering and strategic warning with regard to the possibility of nuclear surprise against the Soviet Union and its East European allies.[25]

The danger of reciprocal alerting of nuclear forces leading to crisis instability was not hypothetical. The Soviet concept of an alerted or generated force might have been entirely different from the U.S. concept. The Soviet conceptual framework for military planning emphasized mobilization, readiness, and concentration of all force components with generating nuclear forces as one part of that process.[26] Soviet political leaders and military planners were disinclined to use nuclear alerts as political signaling devices during a crisis. Their view was that crisis was an objective condition or period of threat during which states actually prepare for war.[27] Additionally, skewing of intelligence and warning toward the extreme case of "bolt from the blue" attacks may have been less pronounced in Soviet nuclear planning compared with American. Although Soviet historical experience emphasized the importance of avoiding strategic military surprise, the totally unexpected and massive surprise nuclear strike was not judged as the most probable by Soviet military thinkers of the 1970s and subsequently. The Voroshilov materials confirm this, as does Soviet force deployments and crisis management behaviors.[28] With improved political relations and more diverse and survivable deployments, the Soviet Union of the 1950s and 1960s became less convinced of its strategic nuclear inferiority. The political leadership would have expected to receive from various intelligence sources at least some advance warning of any hostile intent to attack, and this warning would allow some time to prepare a response. Moreover, if the Soviet Union could attain strategic nuclear parity with the United States, Soviet leadership gained options of preemption, launch under attack/launch on tactical warning, or second strike ride out.[29]

Strategic warning indicators provided by various Soviet intelligence agencies would have been derived from monitoring of western communications traffic, troop movements, diplomatic initiatives, and any other apparent preparations for higher levels of military alert or for war.[30] The Soviet view of combat readiness recognized that not all forces can be alerted at the same rate or need be. Strategic retaliatory forces, air defense troops, and ground and air forces deployed in the first operational echelon had to be maintained "at full wartime strength and should be able to advance themselves to a level of full combat readiness in the shortest time for the accomplishment of assigned missions."[31] The decision for strategic deployment (*strategicheskoye razvertyvaniye*) and for the transition of the Soviet armed forces from a peacetime to a wartime standing was one to be made by the highest political leadership.[32] According to authoritative Soviet sources, continuous control of the armed forces by use of military communications networks and other links was one of the most important aspects of strategic deployment[33] in order to avoid enemy surprise, communications and command system breakdowns, and subsequent fragmentation of the command system into uncoordinated parts:

> The complex situation in which strategic deployment of the Armed Forces is conducted requires centralized control. At the same time, considering the limited capabilities of control elements to furnish a wide range of timely information and taking into account the possible interruption of control, particularly in a nuclear war, special importance is given to the initiative of commanders at all levels on the basis of overall concepts and plans.[34]

There is little evidence in published Soviet military doctrine to suggest that Soviet armed forces or political leadership would have been interested in fighting a strategic or theater nuclear war (strategic for them) in the controlled and selective manner sometimes envisioned in U.S. academic literature.[35] In the event of nuclear war, Soviet strategic forces "would be used massively rather than sequentially, and against a wide range of nuclear and conventional military targets, command-and-control facilities, centers of political and administrative leadership, economic and industrial facilities, power supplies, etc., rather than more selectively."[36] Urban areas would not have been attacked gratuitously or in pursuit of some arbitrary number of fatalities, but "neither would they be avoided if they were near military, political or industrial targets."[37]

Soviet long-range ballistic missile forces (land based and submarine launched) would not have satisfied the targeting requirements of a cautious Soviet war planner for most of the Cold War. Target arrays in the Transoceanic TVD (Theater of Military Action—essentially North America) would have included both "hard" and "soft" targets. Hard targets are those that are heavily protected and must be attacked by the most accurately delivered warheads, such as missile silos; launch control centers; nuclear weapons storage depots; and other reinforced command, control, communications, and intelligence facilities. Soft targets of interest to Soviet planners were presumably those that destroyed U.S. conventional military power or disabled the U.S. war-related economy: airfields, ports, bases, depots, electric power plants, petroleum refineries, chemical plants related to military use, and other facilities not specially protected against the effects of nuclear blast. A comparison of Soviet targeting requirements for selected years with strategic missile warheads available in the same years against hard and soft targets is provided in Table 1.

After the Cuban Missile Crisis, Soviet political leadership and its NATO opponents recognized that nuclear weapons were not realistically "usable" in battle, although the same weapons could be used for deterrence.[38] This acceptance of mutual deterrence and its underlying arms control construct (strategic nuclear parity) became canonical during the SALT I negotiating period in the late 1960s and early 1970s. Mutual deterrence was a fact of life, from the Soviet standpoint, although not a preferred condition: it did not preclude the possibility of nuclear war.[39] Another marker of the Soviet view of deterrence was Brezhnev's speech at Tula in January 1977 in which the Soviet leader renounced the aim of nuclear superiority as an objective of Soviet policy. Afterward, both political and military leaders consistently acknowledged that Soviet policy was defensive and designed to prevent attacks on the USSR, not for superiority over the United States or for fighting and winning a nuclear war.[40]

The acceptance of mutual deterrence and the renunciation of the value of nuclear superiority also affected the evolving Soviet view of ballistic missile defenses (BMD). More or less taken for granted as desirable components of any credible deterrent posture in the 1950s

Table 1: Soviet Nuclear Targeting

Year	Targets	Warheads Required	Warheads Available	Net, WHA-WHR
SOFT TARGETS				
1960	1,000–1,200	2,000–2,400	10	-1990 -2390
1965	1,000–1,200	2,000–2,400	415	-1585 -1985
1970	1,000–1,200	2,000–2,400	1,440	-560 -960
1980	1,000–1,200	2,000–2,400	2,780	380 780
1985	1,000–1,200	2,000–2,400	3,520	1,120 1,520
HARD TARGETS				
1960	—	—	—	—
1965	1,200	2,400	220*	-2,400
1970	1,200	2,400	230	-2,170
1980	1,200	3,600	4,200**	600
1985	1,200	3,600	4,900	1,300

*Soviet SS-7 and SS-8 ICBMs would not have been effective against hard targets such as Minuteman silos, but they could have been targeted against the softer Atlas and Titan launchers still in the U.S. inventory.

**The 1980 versions of SS-18 and SS-19 Soviet ICBMs would not have been effective against upgraded U.S. Minuteman ICBM silos rated at about 2,000 psi. Thus Soviet countersilo attacks in 1980 would have required much more than the three-on-one targeting that the later SS-18 Mod 4 and the SS-19 Mod 3 made feasible by the mid-1980s.

Source: Adapted from estimates by William T. Lee. See William T. Lee and Richard F. Staar, *Soviet Military Policy since World War II* (Stanford, CA: Stanford University/Hoover Institution Press, 1986), 160.

and 1960s, in the later context of SALT I, missile defenses were described as threatening to arms control and politically destabilizing. After the summer of 1971, the subject of missile defenses disappeared almost entirely from official publications, reappearing only with the onset of controversy over the U.S.-proposed Strategic Defense Initiative in the 1980s. Military publications of the early 1970s that expressed criticism of BMD tended to do so on the basis of its technical difficulties, perhaps related to problems in deploying the Galosh missile defense system in the latter 1960s.[41] The official Soviet Communist Party and government position after 1972 supported compliance with the ABM Treaty of 1972, which relieved the USSR of international parity in BMD technology. Eventual modernization of the Galosh system with improved interceptors and radars in the 1980s made

it essentially equivalent in capability to the U.S. Safeguard generation of BMD, briefly deployed as SALT-permitted protection for ICBM
fields and then retired by the U.S. Congress in 1975.

Soviet military analysts on the General Staff told their political leaders in the Kremlin that the realities of modern war precluded
victory in a large-scale conventional war, such as might occur in
Europe, as well as in any nuclear war. The conventional forces of the
Soviet empire and of NATO, were they to clash on the northern and
central European fronts and somehow avoid escalation to nuclear
attack, would nevertheless destroy the very social values the two
sides were thought to be defending. A repeat of the Second World
War to an acceptable, although costly, outcome was simply not feasible by any measure of military planning. The superfluity of large-
scale conventional warfare was even more threatening to the Soviet
psyche than was the recognition—commonplace among elites by
the latter 1960s and by scientists even earlier—that a nuclear war
would have no winners. The cult of the Great Patriotic War in Russia
bolstered the regime against its many failures in economics and in
public rectitude. If the Red Army was no longer a usable instrument
against the main enemy as defined by Moscow and at an acceptable
cost, why should Soviet citizens continue to tolerate empty stores
and shelves in order to devote 15 percent of their GNP to defense?
Table 2 summarizes indicators of U.S. and Soviet nuclear and conventional military power for selected years of the Cold War.

During the Gorbachev era after 1985, theorists from civilian
research institutes were encouraged to develop concepts of arms
control and "reasonable sufficiency" in defense more in keeping with
Gorbachev's desire to reduce defense expenditures and to stabilize
the arms race.[42] Other defense intellectuals argued that numerical
parity in nuclear arms even at lower levels was insufficient to guarantee stability: managing the problem of inadvertent war or escalation was equally significant.[43] Some authors contended that nuclear
war stood apart from any relationship between war and politics as
previously posited by Clausewitz or Lenin.[44] The agreement to eliminate so-called long-range, intermediate nuclear forces (LRINF) in
Europe, reached by Presidents Reagan and Gorbachev, testified to
the shared recognition of the absurdity of nuclear war and to the
changed perceptions of the two sides' intentions that had taken root
between Reagan's first and second terms in office.

Russia's post-Soviet leadership insistence on adherence to the
ABM Treaty of 1972 showed that the concept of nuclear forbearance
by mutual deterrence had carried forward from the Cold War into an
uncertain future. Post–Cold War U.S.–Russian cooperation on CIS

Table 2: U.S. and Soviet Force Levels, Selected Years

System	1964		1968		1972		1976		Change 1964–1976				1980	
									Amount		(%)			
	US	USSR	US	USSR	US	USSR	US	USSR	US	USSR	US	USSR	US	USSR
ICBMs	654	200	1,054	700	1,054	1,118	1,054	1,527	400	1,327	(61)	(664)	1,054	1,398
SLBMs	336	20	656	50	656	450	656	845	320	825	(95)	(4,125)	656	950
Bombers	630	190	650	250	569	140	387	140	-243	-50	(-39)	(-26)	348	150
Major surface combatant ships	300	200	325	200	250	225	175	225	-125	25	(-42)	(13)	175	260
Tactical aircraft	5,700	3,500	5,700	3,500	5,000	4,500	5,000	6,000	-700	2,500	(-12)	(71)	5,000	6,500
Division equivalents[a]	19	7	20	10	16	25	16	25	-3	18	(-16)	(257)	16	27

[a]U.S. and Soviet divisions are not directly comparable. Soviet divisions are made equivalent to those of the United States in this comparison.

Source: Lawrence J. Korb, "Where Did All the Money Go? The 1980s US Defense Buildup and the End of the Cold War," ch. 1 in Stephen J. Cimbala, ed., Mysteries of the Cold War (Aldershot: Ashgate Publishers, 1999), 3–18.

denuclearization, nonproliferation, and a comprehensive test ban (CTB) agreement opened for signature in 1996 suggested that nuclear weapons were viewed differently and excess numbers of them should be discarded.[45] However, as always the case, politics as much as prudence would dictate the timing and character of future nuclear arms reductions. The international system of the twenty-first century evolved so that Russians and Americans, no longer enemies, questioned whether they should work toward mutual deterrence based on assured vulnerability inherited from the Cold War. The role of defenses in post-Soviet Russia remained dependent in uncertain ways on U.S.–Russian arms negotiations, perceived threats to Russia from various points of the compass, and Russia's ability to afford to modernize its nuclear offenses or antinuclear defenses.

Strategic Defense and Military-Technical Innovation

Viable options for fighting below the nuclear threshold were all the more important for Soviet planners in the 1970s and 1980s because Russia's strategically defensive policy (at least from Moscow's point of view) would have to be supported by an improved military capability for assertive conventional military operations against NATO, based in part on a clearer grasp of assertive military defensiveness. Nuclear stalemate at the level of general war thus generated a more careful rethinking of battlefield military strategy while controlling escalation in Soviet favor. The Soviets thus returned to some of their World War II and prewar experience and reanalyzed its significance for modern times.[46]

The great Russian commander and military theorist Aleksandr Suvorov was not enamored of defensive actions. "The very name defense," he once wrote, "already proves weakness, and so it incites timidity."[47] But a Suvorov in command of Soviet forces in the 1970s and 1980s would have recognized that new weapons and command-control systems allowed for more active offensive and defensive battle, below the nuclear threshold. In addition to new technologies, Soviet revisitation of its own World War II history—and influential thinking about operational art by prominent commanders—spurred a new appreciation of defense as a necessity in war planning. Prior to 1985, these modern views of the defensive did not imply lack of unity of politico-military and military-technical levels of Soviet military doctrine: after Gorbachev, reconciliation of the two levels became more problematical.[48]

As early as 1982, Marshal N. V. Ogarkov (then-chief of the Soviet General Staff) had noted that "the previous forms of employment of combined units and formations have in large measure ceased to correspond to present conditions."[49] A new U.S. military strategy, according to Ogarkov, called for "preparing the armed forces to wage a war with the employment of solely conventional weaponry."[50] This contention was repeated by Ogarkov in a 1985 publication. After discussing the nuclear strategy of the Reagan administration as one that emphasized offense with the possibility of a preemptive first strike, Ogarkov noted that the U.S. military strategy "also envisions training its armed forces to wage a war with the use of only conventional means of destruction."[51] An authoritative study of tactics, published in 1984 and edited by Lt. Gen. V. G. Reznichenko, noted,

> The offensive engagement today is more dynamic than in the last war. Being fully motorized and amply equipped with tanks, forces can attack with smaller densities of personnel and equipment than before, and yet in considerably greater depth and with greater momentum.[52]

Using only conventional weapons, the enemy's first and second echelons and reserves could be attacked sequentially while moving rifle and tank subunits deep into the enemy's defense. Modern weaponry use "increases the decisiveness of an offensive engagement"[53] through increased troop capabilities to defeat the enemy without overall superiority in forces and equipment.[54] According to Soviet tactical assessments, modern rifle and tank subunits with highly effective combat equipment and weapons were capable of breaching quickly a deeply echeloned defense even if the defenders were well equipped with nuclear weapons and high-technology conventional forces, including ground-launched antitank weapons, artillery, reconnaissance-strike complexes, airborne and amphibious assault units, and helicopters.[55]

Note that this mid-1980s assessment was offered of Soviet capabilities for conventional weapons only, and its apparent optimism concealed a concern on the part of Soviet planners that in the event of actual war, as opposed to military exercises, these objectives might not be attained. Much depended on correct timing and coordination. Although total surprise against NATO was not probable during any crisis or period of tension, partial surprise was possible. The Soviet Union needed at least partial surprise if it were to have any hope of breaching a fully prepared NATO defense.[56] After the dramatic political events of 1989 in which the fall of communist governments in eastern Europe compromised the Warsaw Pact as a cohesive military alliance, the prospect for a short warning attack against NATO without reinforcement seemed to drop from improbable to impossible, thus compelling the Soviet Union to assume the defensive, not the offensive, in the initial period of war.

Col. Gen. M. A. Gareev, then–deputy chief of the Soviet General Staff, wrote in 1985 that Soviet military theory and operational plans on the eve of World War II gave insufficient attention to the proper conduct of the operational and strategic defensive. He noted that the "idea of the continuous shifting of war at its very outset to enemy territory (and the idea was unsound both scientifically and backed up neither by an analysis of the actual situation or by operational calculations) had so beguiled certain leading military workers that the possibility of conducting military operations on our own territory was virtually excluded."[57] This same assessment was offered by Andrey Kokoshin and Valentin Larionov in their discussion of the battle of Kursk as a model for implementing the doctrine of defensive sufficiency:

> If anything, the Second World War and Hitler's operation Barbarossa should have told the Soviets the virtues of strategic defense. After all, Soviet attempts to conduct deep operations had been a disaster, and the only major victories of the war, such as the battles of Kursk or Stalingrad, had been achieved when the Soviets were forced to take the defensive.[58]

However, the problem of military stability has always been two sided: the prevention of accidental/inadvertent war was as important as the deterrence of deliberate aggression. According to prominent Soviet military theorists of the 1980s, previous military planning did not always take into account all aspects of the complex relationship between mobilization and deterrence. In a departure from the precedent set by V. D. Sokolovskiy's *Voennaya strategiya* (*Military Strategy*) in the 1960s, Gareev in his *M. V. Frunze—voennyi teoretik* (*M. V. Frunze—Military Theorist*) in the mid-1980s doubted whether mobilization of all essential forces and means prior to war was either necessary or desirable.[59] The Sokolovskiy volume reflected the shared conviction by the Soviet military leadership in the 1960s that any war between East and West would shortly become nuclear and all out. By the time of Gareev's *M. V. Frunze,* Soviet theory had changed considerably, beginning with a major priority in 1966 against world war and the nuclear destruction of the USSR.[60]

Prevention of the nuclear destruction of the Soviet Union could not be guaranteed once fighting had expanded to include strikes against the territorial homelands of the superpowers. Even the limited use of nuclear weapons in Europe carried incalculable risks of expansion into total war. Therefore, to the extent possible, escalation to the level of nuclear warfare would have to be forestalled, and the Soviet ground and tactical air forces in Europe would have to fight below the nuclear threshold. Soviet theater and strategic nuclear forces would assume the roles of counterdeterrents to NATO's theater and strategic nuclear deterrents, opening the highway for a conventional test of strength.[61]

Even without nuclear escalation, the problem of military stability and the possibility of first strike fears leading to war demanded further attention. Gareev referred to mobilization as "tantamount to war" in the sense that mobilization sends signals to the other side, raising its level of awareness and raising its sensitivity to any indicators of planning for surprise attack.[62] The Soviet General Staff would have preferred to have authorization for prewar mobilization which was proof even against worst case surprises, but the likelihood is that the post-1985 political leadership would have denied them this.[63] Therefore, the armed forces had to plan for war under disadvantageous conditions and allow for the possibility of enemy preemption with conventional deep strike. According to the guidelines provided by Soviet political leadership (Gorbachev) in the latter 1980s, military doctrine emphasized the prevention (*predotvrashchat'*) of war, and for this purpose the political leadership had to avoid provocative mobilizations inviting enemy preemption.[64] For some Soviet military planners of the latter 1980s, the problem of optimizing preparedness while avoiding unnecessary provocation of potential enemies was a reminder of the months immediately preceding Barbarossa:

> The Soviet leadership did not want to provoke hostilities at a time of complex secrecy in the Soviet system, so that there was a fundamental dysfunction—a cybernetic dysfunction—between two Soviet systems of information. One was among the initiated, and that included a good portion of the General Staff and certainly the political leadership who thought that war was coming, although how close they could not say. The second was an attitude among the rank-and-file that war was not close and therefore should not be anticipated.[65]

For both prospective attackers and defenders using large and technologically well-equipped forces in the last two decades of the Cold War, deterrence rested on the capability for rapid mobilization, as well as concentration and deployment of combat and combat support elements—once war was judged likely. This importance was emphasized in lecture materials from the Soviet General Staff Academy during the 1970s.[66] In addition, modern reconnaissance systems, weapons, and control capabilities allowed the defense to seize the initiative. It was precisely the possibility that NATO could seize the initiative from an initially defensive posture to inflicting deep strikes on Soviet reinforcements and logistics that concerned Soviet planners in the 1980s.

In short, applying current and future weapons technology could overturn the enemy's plans, allow attacks against enemy forces at great depth, and inflict decisive losses *whether fighting from the offensive or the defensive*. The complexity of even small high-technology conventional forces, let alone larger ones, made the struggle for information more important for the defender who must seize the initiative as soon as the prospective attacker's plans are successfully gleaned. However, in an era of nuclear and highly destructive conventional weapons, provocation of an attack that was not actually being planned had to be avoided. The line between deterrence and provocation could be maintained by prospective defenders only if their command and control systems were intact and functioning with high effectiveness.

Under the relentless pressure of modern battle, command and control systems and other aspects of defensive combat stability (*zhivuchest'*) were almost certain to be stressed to the ultimate, even if nuclear escalation could have been avoided. Authoritative Soviet assessments of NATO potential to conduct an "air-land operation" in the latter 1980s warned that the objective of such an operation would be "destroying the enemy throughout the entire depth of his army's operational formation."[67] These conditions of uninterrupted battle emphasized combined arms and three-dimensional combat:

> Defensive combat within the framework of an air-land operation is a combination of static and dynamic actions by combined-arms formations and units, coupled with growing fire pressure upon the advancing, deploying and attacking enemy. It presupposes integrated application of the principles of positional and mobile defense with the purpose of halting an offense and seizing the initiative. In this case *defense is conducted no less decisively than offense* [emphasis added].[68]

In the latter 1980s, Soviet military theory was moving in the direction of integrated offense and defense; it was not declaredly defensive. In an article in the December 1989 issue of *Kommunist,* Soviet defense minister Dmitri Yazov outlined his view of a change in the relationship between the political (or socio-political) and military-technical levels of Soviet military doctrine.[69] Yazov acknowledged that past development of Soviet military doctrine contained a contradiction: politically, its military doctrine was always defensive yet its military-technical reliance was placed on "decisive offensive actions" to forestall war unleashed against the Soviet Union and its allies. It was also assumed that the higher the capability of the Soviet armed forces for such actions, the more solid the defense and the less likely an attack would be initiated by the enemy. Therefore, according to Yazov, "in the contemporary contents of our doctrine, brought into action in 1987, this contradiction is completely eliminated."[70] This was accomplished by movement toward reasonable sufficiency for defense, which would become evident through changes in Soviet defense budgets and in force structure.

Gorbachev's effort to impose defensiveness on Soviet military doctrine was, as we now know, successful only in part.[71] The parlous state of the Soviet economy in the latter 1980s drove Gorbachev to favor nuclear and conventional arms reductions and to redefine East–West competition as a need for common European security cooperation.[72] However, the rapid collapse of the Warsaw Treaty Organization and Soviet control over its former military satellites in east- central Europe closed the debate prematurely over "defensive sufficiency" in favor of matters more urgent. In February 1988, Gorbachev announced that the Limited Contingent of Soviet Forces in Afghanistan would be completely withdrawn within one year. In one sense the Soviet military reduced its negative international reputation when it left Afghanistan; from another standpoint, it suffered a serious blow to its self-esteem. The Soviet army had "lost" a war for the first time, and the setbacks could not be blamed on third-world factions.[73] Military participation in the attempted overthrow of Gorbachev in August 1991 provided additional evidence that some members of the Soviet officer corps had become more politicized in favor of "Soviet" military doctrine than had their nominal party and government civilian superiors.[74] The collapse of the Soviet Union in December 1991 brought a halt to the further development of a uniquely Soviet military theory, strategy, and doctrine, but much of it would be carried forward into the armed forces of newly democratic Russia.

Gorbachev shared with his immediate predecessors, Yuri Andropov and Konstantin Chernenko, distrust of the entire U.S. Strategic Defense Initiative on two grounds: that it was dangerous to political détente even if it did not work and that it was dangerous to deterrence stability if it did work. Gorbachev, in keeping with his more ambitious and reformist agenda at home and abroad, continued in his attempt to redirect Soviet military strategy through his deconstruction of Soviet politics. Turning Leninism inside out, Gorbachev averred that the international class struggle had been superseded by the common problem of preserving international peace and promoting shared human values. Taking away the concept of irrevocable class struggle removed the rationale for Soviet military superiority with respect to its adversaries. Adversaries were enemies of convenience, not ideological opponents. In addition, Gorbachev's "new political thinking" asserted that the first priority in resolving interstate conflicts should be through political—not military—means. Clausewitz's assertion of an indissoluble connection between war and politics made no sense in the nuclear age when a nuclear war could end civilization and society itself, including both socialist and capitalist societies.

Gorbachev, therefore, interpreted missile defense as an effort by the United States to revert to seeking military superiority through means to fight a nuclear war, as well as to deter one. Some Soviet scientists and military thinkers maintained an interest in the BMD option even in the 1980s, but the steadily downward slide of the Soviet economy in that decade precluded the possibility of missile defense beyond the "improved Galosh" stage. Thus, post-Soviet Russia, as the Soviet Union's nuclear and antinuclear successor, would control the destiny of missile defense for the Russian homeland.

Post-Soviet Russia and into the Twenty-First Century

Russian military strategy in the post-Soviet era remains a work in progress. The party-political guidance for developing military strategy during the Soviet era was often arbitrary and abstract, although it provided a high comfort level for military bureaucrats who were willing to accept it. The armed forces were permitted wide latitude on military-technical questions. In a steady state political environment, such as the era of "stagnation" under Brezhnev, the system rewarded stolid compliance and desk-bound inertia. But technology and history were working to undermine this complacency. The apparent placidity of the Brezhnev era was deceptive: the Soviet economy was falling behind the economies of its western competition. That failure was not only a matter of degree (fewer consumer goods available and of less quality) but also was systemic. The West triumphed in the military-technical revolution, and the Soviet military was unable to survive under the pressures brought by Gorbachev's state reform efforts.

The 1990s saw chaos in the government that spread to the armed forces and a reciprocal decline in military effectiveness that reverberated into government crisis. Russia's war in Chechnya from 1994 to 1996 was a military and political disaster. It almost cost Boris Yeltsin his bid for reelection. The prestige of the Russian army was never lower in modern times than it was in the immediate aftermath of its humiliation from Grozny to Pervomaiskoye. Yeltsin's administration ended without having provided for the armed forces a clear and coherent statement of military doctrine or military strategy. Power struggles within the armed forces leadership and various reorganizations of the military and of the other power ministries only introduced additional chaos into Russian security policy in the 1990s, and it became clear that no one was in charge.

Yeltsin had evolved from a communist bureaucrat into a populist politician. His successor, Vladimir Putin, appeared to be again a more traditional bureaucrat. But Putin's personality was one of many layers. His low-key exterior concealed a firmness of purpose and intent that was missing under Yeltsin. Putin concluded, while serving in Yeltsin's shadow as prime minister, that Russia required a more resolved central authority in the Kremlin. Having assumed office, he embarked on political reforms and reorganizations intended to increase the power of the presidential administration and central government while weakening the autonomy of regional governors and local forces. Putin also sought a more direct and personal control over the power ministries that had broken from presidential control under Yeltsin. In this regard, of controlling the military and security bureaucracies, Putin's professional KGB background served him well.

Putin recognized that matters could not be left as they were in Russia's relationship with Chechnya. The war of 1994–1996 had ended with a de facto recognition that Chechnya was an autonomous state within Russia. This was not acceptable to Putin, nor to his generals, who sought another opportunity to put things right in the rebellious republic. In 1999, following an incursion by Chechens into Dagestan and bombings in Moscow blamed on Chechen terrorists by Russians, Putin launched a second Russian campaign against Chechen resistance.

This second campaign was better prepared in both political and military terms than the preceding campaign of 1994–1996. It was also brutally conducted with little or no regard for collateral damage or humanitarian sensibilities. Russian artillery and airpower targeted girds on the map, which infantry and special forces of the interior ministry (OMON) troops would clear and hold the devastated territory.

Russian forces devastated, cleared, and held an area, but Chechen partisans and spies continued to infiltrate Russian lines of control and carry out acts of sabotage and terrorism. By the summer of 2002, the yin and yang of Russian occupation and Chechen resistance had reached a point where Russia was willing to withdraw its regular military forces from the beleaguered republic and declare victory by the end of the year, garrisoning Chechnya with Russian OMON troops and constabulary Chechen formations supporting pro-Russian Chechen politicians.[75]

Whether Russia succeeds in pacifying Chechnya, Russia's military and political leaders understand Russia's inferiority in the so-called Revolution in Military Affairs (RMA). America's primacy in war fighting with advanced C4ISR systems has been beyond dispute since Operation Desert Storm. NATO's Operation Allied Force in 1999 used long-range, precision airpower for political and military coercion of Yugoslavia over Russia's objections and apart from any United Nations approval. Russian military leadership also observed and learned from American military performance in Afghanistan in the fall and winter of 2001. The United States employed an innovative strategy that combined advanced technology for reconnaissance and air warfare with special operations forces, intelligence support, and indigenous ground forces. The rapid demise of the Taliban regime was in contrast to the futility with which Soviet forces sought to subdue rebellious Afghan tribes from 1979 through 1989. Prior to its involvement in Afghanistan, the former Soviet military enjoyed a reputation for invincibility, Afghanistan proved to be a quick "knight's move" for U.S. policy makers and commanders with the limited objectives of regime change and political rebuilding.

Russia's deficiencies in information-based warfare were compounded by the political and economic logjam blocking efforts to reform its military personnel system. U.S. success in Afghanistan and Russia's debacle in Chechnya from 1994 through 1996 both pointed to the importance of smart soldiers in addition to smart technology. A great deal of institutional reform would be required before Russia could field a military force with the training, education, and mindset suitable for postmodern warfare. Some of this reform must take place outside of the military bureaucracy and perhaps outside the Russian government: U.S. technology development in computers and electronics in the 1980s and 1990s, for example, was largely driven by innovations in the private sector, not by government. To reform the military itself for the information age, Russia must improve its technology and change its military mindset.

Neither the Imperial Russian nor the Soviet traditions placed great confidence in the decision-making capacity of the small group or individual. Information and ideas flowed from the top down, not from the bottom up. Severe and even brutal discipline was assumed necessary to create fighting forces out of rank-and-file soldiers. This model of a personnel-heavy army still holds a precious value for many Russian ranking military bureaucrats. Although it is imperative for Russia's future, it may take a generation of new generals before expectations of empowerment for the ordinary recruit may be realized.

There is more than one lesson in the rapid and decisive mauling of Iraq's armed forces by a U.S.-led coalition in forty days and one hundred hours of ground combat in January and February 1991. Iraq fought in the late Soviet style: unmotivated conscript troops coerced forward, top-down command and control from the rear, and inflexible operations and tactics tethered to set-piece scenarios. Iraq was not defeated by smart technology but by smart soldiers and their fast-thinking officers. Operation Desert Storm's information infrastructures and networks were conceived to command and control vast coalition military operations in the Kuwaiti theater of operations and were mostly improvised by local commanders and their technical support teams. Off-the-shelf civilian electronics and communications technology was rewired and adapted for the mission regardless of whether it met military specifications (the infamous MILSPECS). American ingenuity throughout the ranks is what made Operation Desert Storm so one-sided—ingenuity that is cultural, inherent in the social psyche from childhood, and not necessarily transferable to others.

The present predominant challenge for the Russian armed forces, therefore, is developing new military behavioral, or cultural, expectations. These include the possibility of reward for innovative thinking by troops, more decentralized command systems, less punitive treatment of soldiers on a day-to-day basis, and voluntary enlistment instead of conscription as the basis of armed forces recruitment. These goals are attainable provided that Russia's improved relations with the West will open its economy and society to stimuli for innovation. Not only the "hardware" of new technology and equipment is necessary for improving Russian industry and armed forces: equally relevant is the "software" of encouragement and reward for newly empowered warriors. More than ever before: in the twenty-first century the individual soldier *is* the "system" and not the reverse: each trooper is a potentially pivotal force between victory and defeat.

Conclusion

Soviet adaptation to the nuclear age is one of the most instructive and important cases of military transformation in modern times. Soviet leaders were required to make major reassessments in their political ideology, their roles of science and technology in history and in military art, and their relationship between limited and total war. Immense adjustments in military planning and strategic thinking were also required and caused reverberations not only among the military bureaucrats themselves but within the highest ranks of the party and state leadership.

Like American scientists, Russian scientists were tasked during the Cold War to resolve the deadlock of mutual deterrence based on offensive retaliation. One result was that some missile defense interceptors were deployed around Moscow, causing anxiety among members of the U.S. Congress and subsequent demands for a matching ballistic missile defense system. But the Soviet BMD technology was no more reliable than the equally self-defeating American efforts to circumvent the supremacy of offenses in the Cold War years.

During the same period, the Soviets were no more successful than the Americans in repealing the dominance of offensive ballistic missiles over defenses, although they did advance the theory and practical discussion of high technology, conventional warfare below the nuclear threshold. Soviet military literature of the 1980s anticipated the Revolution in Military Affairs that would captivate American military writers and the U.S. research and development community in the 1990s, with the spectacular performance of U.S. technology in the Gulf War as an added propellant. Post-Soviet Russia found itself so far behind NATO in the advanced technologies for twenty-first-century warfare that Russia and NATO reversed strategies compared to the Cold War: Russia emphasized early nuclear use and NATO anticipated using nuclear weapons as a last resort.

3

RUSSIAN NUCLEAR COMMAND AND
CONTROL AND STABLE DETERRENCE

Nuclear command and control systems are as important to arms control and stable deterrence as are the nuclear forces themselves. Some experts have questioned how reliable Russia's nuclear command, control, and communications systems might be.[1] Others fear that if the United States withdraws from the ABM Treaty, missile defense deployments may increase Russia's reliance on hair-trigger alert and prompt launch for its strategic nuclear forces.[2] There is a possible contradiction between American and Russian completion of offensive arms reductions and the Bush administration commitment to deploy antimissile defenses: the smaller the offenses, the more destabilizing even modest defenses might be. Conversely, if deterrence fails, smaller offenses make the task of the defenses easier.

Nuclear Command and Control: Objectives
POSITIVE AND NEGATIVE CONTROL
The first requirement for a strategic nuclear C3 system is the ability to balance the requirements for positive and negative control. Although this can be discussed as two separate requirements, they are intimately related. "Negative control" prevents any nuclear release or launch except by duly authorized command. "Positive control" demonstrates prompt and reliable forces response to authorized commands. In some discussions this is characterized as the "always-never" problem: always ensuring that forces are responsive when required but never permitting actions that are unintended by political or military leaders.[3] However, the term "positive control launch" can cause confusion and misunderstanding because it is actually a form of negative control. Positive control launch, as in SAC Cold War "fail safe" procedures, restrains an attack from taking place unless a

specific coded message authorizes the attack even after bomber aircraft have been loaded with weapons and routed to preliminary airborne destinations.

There is inherent tension between the requirements for negative and positive control at the margin, especially during the alerting of military forces.[4] Nuclear weapons make this tension acute. Steps taken to ready forces for prompt retaliation after enemy attack can remove some of the controls against accidental or unauthorized use. More significant than changes in hardware are shifts in the expectations of military operators who, as a confrontation between two states looms, change from latent to manifest awareness of the worst possible performance of the system for which they are responsible. On one hand, forces will be expected to guard against worst case possibilities. On the other hand, forces and command systems can only be maintained at high alert levels for a remarkably short time before performance degradation sets in and reduces their readiness for war.

If the cost-benefit ratio for alerts is extended beyond the curve midpoint and yields only incremental benefits for ready forces, then deteriorated performance, including performance capable of causing accidents, is a possible outcome. People become fatigued, machinery wears, and nerves fray. Stress levels rise. Interpretations of events are influenced by physical system and human strains. This stress and tension is exacerbated when adding complexity of an attack by one side on the information bytes of the other. One possible result of stress compounded by misinformation is the tendency to rationalize or falsely explain whatever action was recently taken. Another possible result is cognitive or motivational bias in assessments of the status of forces and command and control systems, including information networks.[5] A cognitive bias occurs in the logical explanation for an event or forecast of a future event. Motivational bias occurs when the emotional needs of the observer distort his or her perception of what is being observed.

First strike fears compounded by information malaise and motivational or cognitive bias can also contribute to an outbreak of accidental or inadvertent war. If leaders believe that the opponent will attack at their weakest moment of preparedness and if they are further persuaded that their command system is compromised from enemy disinformation, they may shut down channels or networks that maintain negative control under stressful conditions. Consider, for example, the problem of crisis time communication with ballistic missile submarines (SSBNs). The possible disruption of these communications in time of war and the equally strong possibility of prompt enemy attacks against the other side's SSBN force led Cold War U.S. policy makers to enable submarines to launch their weapons under approved "fail deadly" procedures. This meant that, faced with disrupted communications and under presumed attack from enemy attack submarines, U.S. ballistic missile submarines (under certain restrictive guidelines) might fire at predesignated targets. Permissive action links (PALs), essentially electronic locks that could only be bypassed by encoded messages from the U.S. National Command Authority, were not installed on U.S. SSBNs during the Cold War, although they were in place on land-based and air-delivered weapons.[6]

The U.S. Navy argued that the environment in which maritime operations were carried out precluded PALs or other devices that depended on the fidelity of shore to ship communications in wartime. In addition, the Navy contended that procedural safeguards against accidental or inadvertent war were more important than mechanical or electronic locks. Navy training and tradition were the guarantors against nuclear usurpation.[7] This argument was not entirely self-serving. In the largest sense, the entire U.S. government depends on the training and tradition of its military as the fundamental guarantees of civil supremacy in time of peace or war. The modern military has always had the physical power or capability to overthrow the government but never the inclination since the end of the Civil War.

The problem of accidental or inadvertent escalation of a crisis into war, or of a mistaken decision for nuclear preemption, is more complicated than simple military overthrow of civil power. Slippage of negative control into accidental or inadvertent war or escalation can occur in stages and without any lapse of military loyalty to civil authority. Disjunction between the intent of political leaders and military operators can take place when commanders are carrying out logical procedures under unusual, but possible, conditions.[8] For instance, standard operating procedure of U.S. naval forces during the Cuban Missile Crisis called for the U.S. Navy to force any Soviet submarines within the quarantine line to the surface. Commanders proceeded quite logically from this standpoint to do exactly that, yet neither policy makers nor navy commanders fully appreciated that this could lead to inadvertent escalation and war.[9] Soviet submarines signaled by depth charges might respond not by surfacing as required but by attacking U.S. vessels. At one point in the crisis this was perceived by President Kennedy, who reportedly exclaimed "almost anything but that" when the possibility of military clashes between U.S. forces and Soviet submarines was mentioned.[10]

WARNING AND ATTACK ASSESSMENT

Avoiding accidental or inadvertent nuclear war or mistaken nuclear preemption also requires a valid warning and attack assessment. Leaders must have confidence that they can distinguish between false and true warnings of attack. They must also expect, once having received a valid warning of attack, that they will have time to respond appropriately. U.S. nuclear warning and attack assessment evolved during the Cold War into a tightly coupled system of warning sensors, analysis and fusion centers, communications links, commanders, and command posts. The nerve center of U.S. Cold War warning and assessment was the North American Aerospace Defense Command (NORAD), located in an underground and hardened shelter complex at Cheyenne Mountain, Colorado. NORAD, even after the Cold War, is the chef d'oeuvre of the elaborate U.S. warning system for surprise attack.

The problem of warning is related to the timing and character of response. Warning and response can be analyzed separately, although operational warning and response correlate closely. When developing long-range, nuclear-tipped missiles, U.S. officials were required to consider that the time between the launch of Soviet ICBMs and their detonations in North America would be twenty minutes or less: submarine-launched missiles could arrive even sooner, depending on their targets and launch positions. Warning, therefore, needed to be automated to some extent but without control passing from a human to a machine. In addition, with such short timelines for warning and response, the initial warning decision and the responsive forces should be assigned to different commands. Thus, for example, the United States assigned to NORAD the strategic warning function and to SAC and the Navy the responsive forces and weapons. The function of NORAD was to establish the plausibility of warning within certain parameters and to initiate a series of conferences among political and military leaders.

The problem of mistaken warning and retaliation prompted U.S. Cold War military and political leaders to develop phenomenal redundancy, or "dual phenomenology." Under this system, indicators of a possible attack must be confirmed from more than a single source of input data. For example, if U.S. early warning (DSP) satellites first detected the exhaust plume of land- or sea-based missiles rising from their Soviet points of origin, minutes later, ballistic missile early warning radars (BMEWS) at Fylingdales Moor, England; Thule, Greenland; and Clear, Alaska, would confirm the initial observations by satellite and provide additional details about the size and character of the attack. The United States also deployed specialized radars to detect submarine-launched ballistic missiles, presumably off the Atlantic and Pacific coasts of the continental United States. The presumption of phenomenal redundancy was that even if a single part of system gave erroneous indications or was out of operation at a particular time, the remainder of the system could effectively confirm or disregard that an attack was under way.

Warning having been confirmed by more than one source, the problem of assessment remained. What kind of attack was in progress: was it a massive surprise strike against a comprehensive target set, or was it a "limited" strike intended for coercive purposes with follow-up attacks held in reserve? U.S. and Soviet leaders in the Cold War concentrated on resolving two possible kinds of errors in attack assessment. A Type I error results in a delayed or flawed launch in response to an actual attack. A Type II error results in a premature or mistaken launch when no actual attack is in progress.[11] Type I and Type II error probabilities are relational, and steps taken to minimize the likelihood of one kind of error often increase the probability of the other type of mistaken decision. For example, building in more elaborate and redundant checks against false warning of attack (Type I) may slow down the decision-making process, thereby increasing the chance of a reaction too late for retaliatory forces to carry out their missions.

The problem of valid warning and appropriate response is complicated by the tight coupling of sensors, assessment centers, and response system. Certain high-technology organizations are especially prone, according to sociologist Charles Perrow, to "normal accidents."[12] So-called normal accidents occur in these kinds of organizations when individual component failures cause other components also to fail but in unexpected ways. The result is a systemic dysfunction not anticipated by the designers of the system. Accident-prone, high-technology organizations, according to Perrow, share two attributes: interactive complexity and tight coupling. Interactive complexity increases the frequency of unexpected or seemingly anomalous interactions among the parts, including the human parts. Tight coupling implies parts of the system interact quickly, sequences of activity are invariant—there is only one right way to do things, little organizational "slack" is available to compensate for error, and safety devices, including redundant checks and balances against failure, are limited to those planned for and designed into the system.[13] The Three Mile Island nuclear power disaster, airline crashes, space shuttle malfunctions, electric power grid brownouts, and other normal accidents may be inevitable in organizations dependent on advanced technology and highly interactive parts. This was true of the

Cold War U.S. nuclear warning, assessment, and response systems, which are examples of high-risk, high-technology systems. Yet normal accidents in the U.S. nuclear command and control system were apparently rare, and obviously none were catastrophic.[14]

Three possible explanations exist for how catastrophic failure was avoided in nuclear warning and attack assessment during the Cold War. First, the situation was overdetermined. Even the most dullard national political leadership would search for any way out before authorizing a nuclear attack or a retaliation based on warning of attack. Second, redundancy built into the system ensured against any retaliation based on mistaken warning. Indeed, false warnings became routine during the Cold War for both United States and Soviet organizations charged with warning. Some might argue that the two sides became so habituated to false warning and the low likelihood of actual attack that they dropped their guards. This charge was laid by Gorbachev against the Soviet military after an intrepid West German pilot flew his Cessna aircraft into Red Square, through and under Soviet radar nets and interceptor squadrons. U.S. military leaders were not lulled into complacency about the possibility of accidental nuclear war. But evidence suggests that their confidence in the decision-making process to compensate for errors in warning and attack assessment—possibly contributory to accidental nuclear war—was excessive.[15]

A third possible explanation is that the United States and the Soviets were simply fortunate that no lethal combination of mistaken warning *and* a nuclear crisis occurred simultaneously. The interactive complexity of both sides' warning systems was never fully tested. Paul Bracken makes the related and significant point that the interaction between the American warning and assessment system *and* its Soviet counterpart became a separate and dangerous part of the Cold War nuclear complex. Both sides watched one another watching. Each interactively complex system reacted to the other and by doing so considerably escalated the possibility of an inadvertent nuclear attack.

DELEGATION OF AUTHORITY

A third requirement for strategic nuclear command and control systems is correct delegation of authority and devolution of command.

The president, as head of the executive branch of the U.S. government, may delegate any of his responsibilities almost without limit. The U.S. Constitution and the Presidential Succession Act of 1947 have established a constitutional order of succession in case of presidential death, disability, or removal from office. The vice president stands at the head of this order of succession, followed by the speaker of the House of Representatives and the president pro tempore of the Senate. After that, the heads of cabinet departments are enumerated from the oldest department to the youngest: State, Treasury, Defense (War originally), and so forth. The president is the only lawful person who can authorize nuclear release to force commanders and retaliatory attacks using nuclear weapons. However, the president is not a singular actor in this regard: he requires cooperation from various other levels of command and responsibility. This need for more than a singular center of competency for nuclear decision, in case of presidential death or disability, overlaps the military *chain of command* with the civilian *chain of succession* in nuclear matters.

The death of a president or even the entire civilian political leadership in a surprise strike on Washington, D.C., cannot be permitted to paralyze U.S. retaliation, for the obvious reason that such vulnerability might invite attack. Therefore, predelegated or devolved command arrangements for nuclear *authorization* (or authentication) and *enablement* must be possible from other sources in extremis. Authorization means that the person or office conveying a command to a subordinate unit is lawfully entitled to do so. Enablement provides the necessary release mechanisms that allow operators to circumvent mechanical or electronic locks assigned to weapons in peacetime to prevent accidental or unauthorized use.[16] For example, an authorization code from the "football" or suitcase carried by a presidential aide tells the receiver that the president has, indeed, sent the indicated command. Enabling commands include the "unlock" codes to bypass electronic locks such as PALs or other use control devices.

Devolution is a complicated matter because—at least in the U.S. Cold War case—authorization and enablement codes were usually not held by the same people or at the same levels of command. The president and the secretary of defense, for example, can authorize nuclear release, but they have neither physical possession nor effective custody of nuclear weapons. Possession is related to custody but not necessarily identical to it. Custody implies control over the weapon, whether in one's possession or not. For example, tactical nuclear weapons may be deployed in storage sites guarded by personnel other than those who would actually use those weapons once authorized and enabled to do so. In theory, authorization and enablement commands would be unambiguous and those lower on the chain of command should automatically carry out orders from higher echelons. The matter is not so simple in practice: human operators, not automatons, are in the chain of command. And actual custody or physical possession of the weapons is the responsibility of lower echelons that are, in any military situation, capable of resistance of various kinds in response to orders. All personnel have some discretion and may decide to change what needs to be changed and to think for themselves once nuclear charges begin to move from storage sites to launch platforms.[17]

As orders cascade downward and outward through bureaucracy, honest misconstructions and organizational self-interest inevitably coexist in crisis-time mobilization. Organizations will do what they have been prepared to do: thus, nuclear force commanders will follow orders to retaliate without questioning their own actions. This model works for a situation of unambiguous clarity: warheads have begun detonating on U.S. soil, the president has identified the transgressor and authorized retaliation, and public support for nuclear response can be assumed. Prior to the actual arrival of nuclear destruction on American targets, the expectations become more confused within and among bureaucratic compartments. One can imagine some elements taking the "wait and see" position given the Cold War history of false alarms. Other elements might delay response and demand additional authentication for so significant an order. Psychological paralysis in the face of orders would be predictable and entirely human, knowing that to unleash nuclear death and destruction places family members at risk from enemy strikes of a similar kind. Table 1 depicts various loci in the Russian and U.S. nuclear command and control systems by function and tabulates their respective influence.

The U.S. nuclear command system works, according to one expert analyst, like a revolver. The function of the presidential center is "not to act *as a trigger to launch nuclear weapons*, but as a *safety catch preventing other triggers from firing*."[18] In time of peace and relaxed tension, the trigger safety is "on" so that the weapon cannot be fired: negative control reigns supreme. As a crisis develops, the controls are progressively relaxed to permit faster reaction to emergency: positive control becomes more important. This process is reflected in the U.S. DefCon gradations for management of alerts: from Level 5 (lowest, peacetime conditions) to Level 1 (highest, ready for imminent war). As policy makers authorize the military to proceed from lower to higher levels of alert, restraints on force movement and preparedness are "unwrapped," and the criterion of readiness for combat takes precedence over peacetime safety and security. Alert management requires expertise, and the United States, even with as much experience as any other country, had its own share of

Table 1: U.S. and Russian Nuclear C3: Command Functions and Capabilities

	AUTHORITY (lawful source of command for nuclear release)	VETO (effective ability to nullify orders from authorities)	PHYSICAL CAPABILITY (effective ability to use weapons and/or launch vehicles)
Constitutional authorities/ U.S. president and secretary of defense/ Russian Federation president and defense minister	yes	no	no
Enabling code holders * U.S. and Russian nuclear CINCs	no, unless authority is predelegated	yes	no
Authorizing code holders ** U.S. Joint Chiefs of Staff/ Russian General Staff	no, unless authority is predelegated	no	possible, if they also hold enabling codes and can transmit an apparently authentic order down the chain of command
Weapon holders/U.S. and Russian air and missile forces, plus custodial units in charge of weapons storage in peacetime	no, unless authority is predelegated	yes	possible, if weapons lack use control devices or if codes have already been given out

*Some levels of command may hold authorization codes as well, for example, commanders in chief of unified and specified commands in the American or Russian General Staff and nuclear CINCs in Russia.
**Some levels of command may hold enablement codes as well, for example, commanders in chief of unified and specified commands or the General Staff and nuclear CINCs in Russia.

Sources: Peter Douglas Feaver, *Guarding the Guardians: Civilian Control of Nuclear Weapons in the United States* (Ithaca, NY: Cornell University Press, 1992); Bruce G. Blair, *The Logic of Accidental Nuclear War* (Washington, DC: Brookings Institution, 1993), 82–86 and 95–96; and Peter Vincent Pry, *War Scare: Russia and America on the Nuclear Brink* (Westport, CT: Praeger, 1999). For checks and balances in the former Soviet nuclear C3 system, see Ibid., 82, and passim.

snafus despite high levels of military personnel reliability and numerous checks and balances in the system.

The former Soviet nuclear C3 system had a number of built-in checks and balances against any accidental nuclear release or, for obvious reasons, against political usurpation of authority. There were also protections against impetuous behavior from one or more levels of command. For a decision to launch nuclear weapons to be taken and followed through to conclusion, all senior military and political leaders representing different departments or arms of service must assent. In addition, the command and control system divided responsibility for the technical maintenance of the nuclear forces from the responsibility for combat command of those forces. The General Staff was normally responsible for the former and the nuclear CINCs for the latter.[19] The abortive coup of 1991 would have been more terrifying except that the power of Soviet leaders to authorize a nuclear attack did not equal the control necessary to implement such an order. Thus, the nuclear CINCs of the Strategic Rocket Forces and other nuclear-capable arms of service essentially resisted any launch commands from the "Extraordinary Committee" of coup plotters.

Conversely, the Soviet nuclear command and control system was not paralyzed during the coup. If necessary, even under attack, the system could have provided for prompt retaliation:

> In the event of enemy nuclear attack the CGS and CINC SRF (Chief of the General Staff and Commander-in-Chief of the Strategic Rocket Forces) still had the capability to generate the requisite preliminary and direct codes. Together they could have disseminated the launch authorization and unlock codes. Alternatively, the command system might have switched over to the automatic mode of operation in the event of an enemy attack that had inflicted severe damage to the chain of command.[20]

The extent to which the present-day Russian nuclear C3 system has the same complex interdependence of checks and balances as the former Soviet one is speculative. It cannot be reassuring for Russian commanders that their nuclear retaliatory forces are much less capable than their former Soviet counterparts, nor that they are backed up by less comprehensive radar and satellite early warning systems against nuclear attack.

Threat Perceptions and Strategic Expectations

For the case of the Russian strategic nuclear command and control system, the problem of error interdependency and its relationship to possible catastrophe is important because Russian military planners and political leaders already feel acutely threatened. The post–Cold War economic aftershock has created deficits in their early warning radar network. Reportedly, Russia has no satellite coverage of the oceans and must depend on allies for warning of any U.S. submarine-launched ballistic missile (SLBM) attack on Russian territory. Because of lack of funds, obsolete communications and computer equipment required for the control of nuclear forces have not been modernized: one result may have been more false signals transmitted by the system during the last few years. In addition, service personnel in the Russian armed forces have endured slow pay and inadequate housing. The subsequent reduced morale has led, in at least one case, to a walkout by the staff of the institute that had designed the nuclear control and communications for the former Soviet and now Russian strategic nuclear forces. Bruce G. Blair is a U.S. expert on the subject of nuclear command and control who is familiar with the problems of Soviet and Russian nuclear C3:

How close has Russia slipped to the edge of a failure, a serious catastrophic failure of command and control? It's really not possible to calculate, but we know the trends are adverse. And we know, I believe, that it's only reasonable that the command system cannot endure this stress indefinitely.[21]

Russian nuclear war-fighting units are breaking down, and repairs are neglected or omitted. The following training and maintenance shortfalls in nuclear units are among their recently documented shortcomings:

1. The Russian navy has difficulty keeping even one or two of its fleet of twenty-six ballistic missile submarines on patrol at the same time—sometimes there are none on patrol.
2. The Strategic Rocket Forces (essentially the land-based missile forces, lately regrouped into a larger strategic forces unit) have considerable difficulty dispersing a single regiment of mobile rockets into their covert field locations.
3. Russian bomber pilots typically receive only about twenty hours of flight training per year (comparable U.S. pilots receive hundreds of hours).
4. Underground nuclear command posts are crumbling owing to lack of maintenance and repair.
5. Laboratories responsible for designing nuclear weapons, building underground command posts, and engineering communications links that send the "go" code to land-based missile forces are virtually bankrupt.
6. According to some sources, even the nuclear "footballs" or suitcases that accompany the Russian president and other members of the High Command are in need of repair.[22]

In addition to these factors tending to raise the random probability of Russian error synergy in a nuclear crisis, Russian (and former Soviet) military planning guidance and doctrine tends to rely on prompt launch (launch on warning) in case of presumed nuclear attack on Russia. Launch on warning means that Russian retaliatory forces would be launched in response to reliable detection of any missile attack but before the attacking missiles and their re-entry vehicles had reached their intended targets in Russia. Launch on warning is a more time-urgent choice for political and military leaders compared to launch after riding out a first strike, which allows leaders more time to validate and authenticate the attack. Launch on warning increases the likelihood of a mistaken decision for retaliation (based on a false or mischaracterized warning) so that retaliatory options based on the circumstances are limited.

How dependent for survival is Russia compared with the United States on preemption or on launch on warning (or launch under attack, a delayed variation of launch on warning)? Related to this is the question of the two states' relative dependence on early alerting or generation of nuclear forces in a crisis, compared to leaving the same forces in their normal peacetime, or day-to-day, condition. To interrogate this problem, we use a nuclear exchange model to calculate the numbers of surviving and retaliating warheads for Russia and for the United States under various assumptions about their alertness and launch doctrines. Each side's forces can be postured in one of four conditions:

> *Maximum retaliation*: generated alert, launch on warning of attack
> *Intermediate retaliation*: generated alert, ride out the attack and then retaliate
> *Intermediate retaliation*: day-to-day alert, launch on warning.
> *Minimum or assured retaliation*: day-to-day alert, ride out the attack

To test the performance of each side's forces under each of these conditions, we hypothesized four possible force structures consistent with the Bush–Putin arms reduction agreement of May 2002 (the Moscow Treaty), within the lower bound (1,700) and high end (2,200) of deployed warheads permitted under the treaty.

> *United States*
> Balanced Triad
> No ICBMs
> No Bombers
> SLBMs Only
>
> *Russia*
> Balanced Triad
> No Bombers
> No SLBMs
> ICBMs Only

Our methodology calculates the numbers of surviving and retaliating warheads for each force, testing each force structure under the previously noted four conditions of alertness and launch doctrine. Table 2 summarizes the results for Russian and U.S. forces within a 2,200 limit; Table 3 provides similar information for forces at the lower limit of 1,700.

The results summarized in Table 2 and Table 3 show that generation stability is high for both the Russian and American forces under conditions of prompt launch, but delayed launch puts much more of a premium on the Russians to generate their forces early in a crisis. In terms of prompt launch stability, Russian forces are more dependent on launch on warning than American forces are, although less so, on generated alert compared with day-to-day alert. These findings about Russia's greater dependency on prompt launch and on force generation hold true across Russia's four different types of hypothetical forces, although not equally so. Some of Russia's Moscow Treaty compatible forces are less dependent on prompt launch or generated alert than others.

None of these findings suggests that the Russian leadership, any more than the American, expects a political crisis capable of leading into a nuclear war. The post–Soviet U.S.–Russian security dialogue since the terrorist attacks on America of September 11, 2001, are almost entirely in a positive direction, even considering

Table 2: U.S. and Russian Surviving and Retaliating Warheads 2,200 Warhead Limit

	Gen/LOW	Gen/RO	Day/LOW	Day/RO
U.S. Forces				
Balanced Triad	842	702	561	421
No Bombers	1086	905	724	543
No ICBMs	988	823	659	494
SLBMs Only	1218	1015	812	609
Russian Forces				
Balanced Triad	730	608	486	365
No Bombers	812	677	541	406
No SLBMs	508	423	338	254
ICBMs Only	786	655	524	393

Source: Author, based on an analytical model first developed by Dr. James J. Tritten. Dr. Tritten is not responsible for its application here.

Table 3: U.S. and Russian Surviving and Retaliating Warheads
1,700 Warhead Limit

	Gen/LOW	Gen/RO	Day/LOW	Day/RO
U.S. Forces				
Balanced Triad	653	544	435	326
No Bombers	802	668	534	401
No ICBMs	799	665	532	399
SLBMs Only	948	790	632	474
Russian Forces				
Balanced Triad	561	468	374	280
No Bombers	689	574	459	344
No SLBMs	491	409	327	245
ICBMs Only	729	608	486	364

Source: Author

some fluctuation. Few plausible circumstances could be imagined that would lead either side into a deliberate nuclear attack on the other. A more disturbing possibility is a desperate set of Russian policy makers who are confused about what is appearing on radar warning screens and uncertain about U.S. intentions, as they might be in a crisis. In this sense, U.S. policy makers have a serious interest in an improved Russian C3 system that can separate correct signals from background "noise" and in one that can provide unambiguous interpretation of the fog of war, or at least, of crisis leading to war. As Blair has noted, the deterioration of the Russian early warning system is a special problem in this regard:

> This progressive deterioration increases the risks of mistaken, illicit or accidental launch and of the loss of strict control over Russia's vast nuclear complex. One need only consider that a degraded early warning network not only loses some ability to detect an actual attack, it simultaneously loses some ability to screen out false indications of attack generated by the sensor network.[23]

Defenses and Command-Control

How could missile defenses influence this Russian mindset? There are two possibilities. First, if missile defenses are deployed jointly by the Russians and the Americans, are limited in size and capability, and are accompanied by offensive arms reductions, then missile defenses could contribute to improved stability (assuming that the political climate remains favorable). However, if offensive arms reductions falter, missile defenses are deployed only by the Americans, and defenses advance much faster technologically than before, then defenses contribute to Russian first-strike fears.

NMD also has immediate implications for Russia's willingness to fulfill its obligations under the Moscow Treaty of May 2002. If Russia foresees no immediate U.S. breakthrough in missile defenses, it can proceed with equanimity to downsize its offensive forces to the lower end of the required range of 1,700 to 2,200. But if Russia anticipates a significant U.S. technology breakthrough in NMD between now and 2012, then it might remove additional warheads from storage or resort to MIRVing part of its ICBM force and prefer the upper treaty limit. During his visit to Washington in November 2001, President Putin stated his preference for reducing both states' arsenals to a maximum of 1,500 warheads: he also indicated Russia would use this number as its planning parameter, regardless of the consequences. The Moscow Treaty of 2002 satisfied Putin's essential plan while allowing the United States some flexibility for warheads demanded by Pentagon planners to fulfill strike plans.

One question on the minds of Russian defense planners would be: how many of their surviving and retaliating warheads might get through U.S. defenses after a U.S. first strike? This number of surviving and penetrating Russian warheads would vary with the effectiveness of U.S. defenses. In Figures 1 through 4, we compare the numbers of surviving and retaliating Russian warheads against four hypothetical levels of U.S. defense effectiveness (Phases I through IV defenses, each adding a layer to the defense that "thins out" or subtracts an additional 20 percent of the other side's retaliation). The same figures also show the estimated numbers of surviving and retaliating U.S. warheads against a similar range of possible Russian defense competencies. Each state's forces were based on a maximum deployment of 2,200 warheads. Four different Russian forces are tested against U.S. defenses: a U.S. balanced triad is used for comparison with Russian forces in each case. A generic template of launch doctrine and alertness for each side's forces is assumed, based on experience.

In the absence of effective defenses, either the United States or Russia can assuredly inflict unacceptable and historically unprecedented damage in a retaliatory strike. However, introducing defenses into the equation creates uncertainties based on the actual effectiveness of

Figure 1

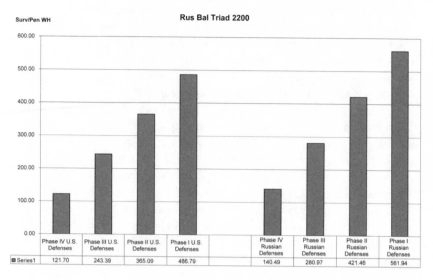

Figure 2

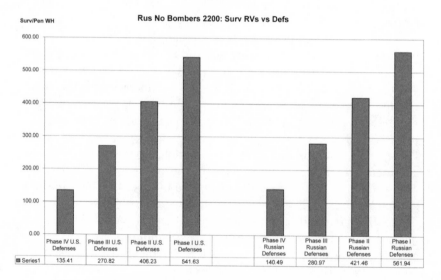

the defenses, the *expected* or projected effectiveness of the defenses (by both first striker and retaliator), and whether defenses are possessed by one or by both sides. In the preceding hypothetical example both sides did possess defenses, but Russians have also to plan for the contingency that the United States alone would be deploying defenses.

Figure 3

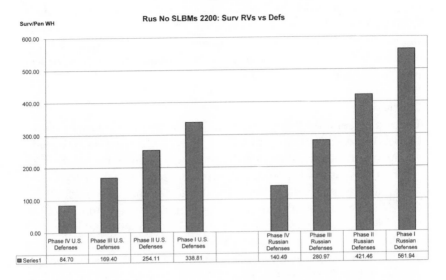

Surv/Pen WH

Rus No SLBMs 2200: Surv RVs vs Defs

	Phase IV U.S. Defenses	Phase III U.S. Defenses	Phase II U.S. Defenses	Phase I U.S. Defenses		Phase IV Russian Defenses	Phase III Russian Defenses	Phase II Russian Defenses	Phase I Russian Defenses
Series1	84.70	169.40	254.11	338.81		140.49	280.97	421.46	561.94

Figure 4

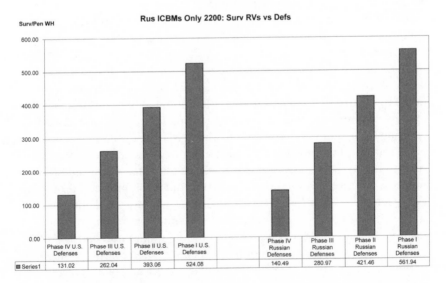

Surv/Pen WH

Rus ICBMs Only 2200: Surv RVs vs Defs

	Phase IV U.S. Defenses	Phase III U.S. Defenses	Phase II U.S. Defenses	Phase I U.S. Defenses		Phase IV Russian Defenses	Phase III Russian Defenses	Phase II Russian Defenses	Phase I Russian Defenses
Series1	131.02	262.04	393.06	524.08		140.49	280.97	421.46	561.94

The preceding example makes the point that mixing deterrence by denial with deterrence by threat of punishment does not necessarily result in better, in other words more reliable, deterrence. Adding deterrence by denial to an existing relationship based on deterrence by threat of unacceptable punishment creates a new universe of unknowns and new kinds of uncertainties. Faced with additional uncertainties, military planners and political leaders might be more reliant on high alert levels in peacetime and on hair-trigger reactions to presumed warning of attack. Defenses could reduce instead of increase the comfort zone of deterrence if command and control is itself uncertain.

Conclusions

There is no apparent imminent risk of command usurpation by unauthorized and disgruntled military in Russia. And Russia has made serious efforts in the past decade, although perhaps not enough, to rebuild the ramshackle post-Soviet architecture of its nuclear command and control system. But, compared to the Soviet nuclear command and control system, Russia's current C3 system is less redundant against isolated errors and more prone to systemic failure possibly leading to accidental or inadvertent war. Russia's first strike fears may have more to do with political encirclement than they do with the technical character of Russia's forces or C3 systems. Care must be taken in future decisions about the enlargement of NATO and/or in avoiding the appearance of demonstrative support for hostile states or nonstate actors within, or near, Russia's borders. Russia's security perceptions include threats from within and without its borders, and these perceptions are based on some realistic recognition of Russia's military weaknesses.

What can the United States do with regard to command stability in Russia? Options do exist. First, it can provide technical assistance to ensure that C3 equipment—including cyber equipment—is modernized and capable of carrying the load. Second, shared early warning information is vital so that the crisis-time commanders depend not on perception but on hard data to reassure them that no real attack is in progress. Third, the United States can reduce the numbers of nuclear weapons inventories and implementation of the Comprehensive Test Ban (CTB) Agreement, which would contribute to the shared interest of Russian and U.S. nuclear nonproliferation. Last, it should consider Russia's decrepit command and control system and the potential interaction between command-control incompetence and defenses that by themselves could act as a deterrent.

Appendix
U.S. AND RUSSIAN STRATEGIC NUCLEAR FORCES

2,200 Warhead Limit

Russian Forces

Balanced Triad

Russian Forces	Launchers	Warheads @	Total Warheads
SS-11/3	0	1	0
SS-13/2	0	1	0
SS-17	0	1	0
SS-25 silo	200	1	200
SS-19/3	0	1	0
SS-27 mobile	150	1	15
subtotal fixed land	350		350
SS-25 (road)	250	1	250
SS-27 (road)	200	1	20
subtotal mobile land	450		45
subtotal land-based	800		800
SS-N-6/3	0	1	0
SS-N-8/2	0	1	0
SS-N-18/2	0	1	0
SS-N-X	112	6	672
SS-N-23	48	3	144
subtotal sea-based	160		816
Tu-95 H 6 / ALCM	0	6	0
Tu-95 H 16	30	16	480
Tu-160 Blackjack	12	8	96
subtotal air-breathing	42	576	
total Russian forces	1002		2192

No Bombers

Russian Forces	Launchers	Warheads @	Total Warheads
SS-11/3	0	1	0
SS-13/2	0	1	0
SS-17	0	1	0
SS-25 silo	200	1	200
SS-19/3	100	3	300
SS-27 mobile	200	1	20
subtotal fixed land	500		700
SS-25 (road)	250	1	250

	Launchers	Warheads @	Total Warheads
SS-27 (road)	200	1	200
subtotal mobile land	450		450
subtotal land-based	950		1150
SS-N-6/3	0	1	0
SS-N-8/2	0	1	0
SS-N-18/2	0	1	0
SS-N-X	128	5	640
SS-N-23	80	5	40
subtotal sea-based	208		1040
Tu-95 H 6 / ALCM	0	6	0
Tu-95 H 16	0	16	0
Tu-160 Blackjack	0	8	0
subtotal air-breathing	0		0
total Russian forces	1158		2190

No SLBMs

Russian Forces	Launchers	Warheads @	Total Warheads
SS-11/3	0	1	0
SS-13/2	0	1	0
SS-17	0	1	0
SS-25 silo	250	1	250
SS-19/3	150	3	450
SS-27 mobile	200	1	200
subtotal fixed land	600		900
SS-25 (road)	250	1	250
SS-27 (road)	200	1	200
subtotal mobile land	450		450
subtotal land-based	1050		1350
SS-N-6/3	0	1	0
SS-N-8/2	0	1	0
SS-N-18/2	0	1	0
SS-N-X	0	6	0
SS-N-23	0	3	0
subtotal sea-based	0		0
Tu-95 H 6 / ALCM	0	6	0
Tu-95 H 16	44	16	704
Tu-160 Blackjack	12	8	96
subtotal air-breathing	56		800
total Russian forces	1106		2150

ICBMs Only

Russian Forces	Launchers	Warheads @	Total Warheads
SS-11/3	0	1	0

SS-13/2	0	1	0
SS-17	0	1	0
SS-25 silo	200	3	600
SS-19/3	150	3	450
SS-27 mobile	250	1	250
subtotal fixed land	600		1300
SS-25 (road)	250	1	250
SS-27 (road)	200	3	600
subtotal mobile land	450		850
subtotal land-based	1050		215
SS-N-6/3	0	1	0
SS-N-8/2	0	1	0
SS-N-18/2	0	1	0
SS-N-X	0	6	0
SS-N-23	0	3	0
subtotal sea-based	0		0
Tu-95 H 6 / ALCM	0	6	0
Tu-95 H 16	0	16	0
Tu-160 Blackjack	0	8	0
subtotal air-breathing	0		0
total Russian forces	1050		2150

U.S. Forces

Balanced Triad

U.S. Forces	Launchers	Warheads @	Total Warheads
Minuteman II	0	1	0
Minuteman III	0	1	0
Minuteman IIIA	300	1	300
Peacekeeper MX	0	10	0
subtotal land-based	300		300
Trident C-4	0	4	0
Trident D-5/W-76	0	4	0
Trident D-5/W-88	336	4	1344
subtotal sea-based	336		1344
B-52G gravity	0	0	0
B-52G gravity	0	0	0
ALCM		0	0
B-52H ALCM	24	12	288
B-2	20	12	240
subtotal air-breathing	44		528
total U.S. forces	680		2172

No Bombers

U.S. Forces	Launchers	Warheads @	Total Warheads
Minuteman II	0	1	0
Minuteman III	0	1	0
Minuteman IIIA	300	1	300
Peacekeeper MX	0	10	0
subtotal land-based	300		300
Trident C-4	0	4	0
Trident D-5/I	168	6	1008
Trident D-5/II	168	5	840
subtotal sea-based	336		1848
B-52G gravity	0	0	0
B-52G gravity	0	0	0
ALCM		0	0
B-52H ALCM	0	12	0
B-2	0	12	0
subtotal air-breathing	0		0
total U.S. forces	636		2148

No ICBMs

U.S. Forces	Launchers	Warheads @	Total Warheads
Minuteman II	0	1	0
Minuteman III	0	1	0
Minuteman IIIA	0	1	0
Peacekeeper MX	0	10	0
subtotal land-based	0		0
Trident C-4	0	4	0
Trident D-5/W-76	0	4	0
Trident D-5/W-88	336	5	1680
subtotal sea-based	336		1680
B-52G gravity	0	0	0
B-52G gravity	0	0	0
ALCM		0	0
B-52H ALCM	22	12	264
B-2	20	12	240
subtotal air-breathing	42		504
total U.S. forces	378		2184

SLBMs Only

U.S. Forces	Launchers	Warheads @	Total Warheads
Minuteman II	0	1	0
Minuteman III	0	1	0
Minuteman IIIA	0	1	0

Peacekeeper MX	0	10	0
subtotal land-based	0		0
Trident C-4	0	4	0
Trident D-5/I	144	7	1008
Trident D-5/II	192	6	1152
subtotal sea-based	336		2160
B-52G gravity	0	0	0
B-52G gravity	0	0	0
ALCM		0	0
B-52H ALCM	0	12	0
B-2	0	12	0
subtotal air-breathing	0		0
total U.S. forces	336		2160

1,700 Warhead Limit

Russian Forces

Balanced Triad

Russian Forces	Launchers	Warheads @	Total Warheads
SS-11/3	0	1	0
SS-13/2	0	1	0
SS-17	0	1	0
SS-25 silo	100	1	100
SS-19/3	0	1	0
SS-27 mobile	150	1	150
subtotal fixed land	250		250
SS-25 (road)	250	1	250
SS-27 (road)	100	1	100
subtotal mobile land	350		350
subtotal land-based	600		600
SS-N-6/3	0	1	0
SS-N-8/2	0	1	0
SS-N-18/2	0	1	0
SS-N-X	80	6	480
SS-N-23	48	3	144
subtotal sea-based	128		624
Tu-95 H 6 / ALCM	0	6	0
Tu-95 H 16	22	16	352
Tu-160 Blackjack	12	8	96
subtotal air-breathing	34		448
total Russian forces	762		1672

No Bombers

Russian Forces	Launchers	Warheads @	Total Warheads
SS-11/3	0	1	0
SS-13/2	0	1	0
SS-17	0	1	0
SS-25 silo	200	1	200
SS-19/3	0	1	0
SS-27 mobile	150	1	150
subtotal fixed land	350		350
SS-25 (road)	250	1	250
SS-27 (road)	200	1	200
subtotal mobile land	450		450
subtotal land-based	800		800
SS-N-6/3	0	1	0
SS-N-8/2	0	1	0
SS-N-18/2	0	1	0
SS-N-X	96	6	576
SS-N-23	64	4	256
subtotal sea-based	160		832
Tu-95 H 6 / ALCM	0	6	0
Tu-95 H 16	0	16	0
Tu-160 Blackjack	0	8	0
subtotal air-breathing	0		0
total Russian forces	960		1632

No SLBMs

Russian Forces	Launchers	Warheads @	Total Warheads
SS-11/3	0	1	0
SS-13/2	0	1	0
SS-17	0	1	0
SS-25 silo	200	1	200
SS-19/3	100	3	300
SS-27 mobile	200	1	200
subtotal fixed land	500		700
SS-25 (road)	300	1	300
SS-27 (road)	200	1	200
subtotal mobile land	500		500
subtotal land-based	1000		1200
SS-N-6/3	0	1	0
SS-N-8/2	0	1	0
SS-N-18/2	0	1	0
SS-N-X	0	6	0
SS-N-23	0	3	

subtotal sea-based	0		0
Tu-95 H 6 / ALCM	0	6	0
Tu-95 H 16	22	16	352
Tu-160 Blackjack	12	8	96
subtotal air-breathing	34		448
total Russian forces	1034		1648

ICBMs Only

Russian Forces	Launchers	Warheads @	Total Warheads
SS-11/3	0	1	0
SS-13/2	0	1	0
SS-17	0	1	0
SS-25 silo	200	1	200
SS-19/3	150	3	450
SS-27 mobile	200	1	200
subtotal fixed land	550		850
SS-25 (road)	250	1	250
SS-27 (road)	200	3	600
subtotal mobile land	450		850
subtotal land-based	1000		1700
SS-N-6/3	0	1	0
SS-N-8/2	0	1	0
SS-N-18/2	0	1	0
SS-N-X	0	6	0
SS-N-23	0	3	0
subtotal sea-based	0		0
Tu-95 H 6 / ALCM	0	6	0
Tu-95 H 16	0	16	0
Tu-160 Blackjack	0	8	0
subtotal air-breathing	0		0
total Russian forces	1000		1700

U.S. Forces

Balanced Triad

U.S. Forces	Launchers	Warheads @	Total Warheads
Minuteman II	0	1	0
Minuteman III	0	1	0
Minuteman IIIA	300	1	300
Peacekeeper MX	0	10	0
subtotal land-based	300		300
Trident C-4	0	4	0

Trident D-5/W-76	0	4	0
Trident D-5/W-88	336	3	1008
subtotal sea-based	336		1008
B-52G gravity	0	0	0
B-52G gravity	0	0	0
ALCM		0	0
B-52H ALCM	9	12	108
B-2	20	12	240
subtotal air-breathing	29		348
total U.S. forces	665		1656

No Bombers

U.S. Forces	Launchers	Warheads @	Total Warheads
Minuteman II	0	1	0
Minuteman III	0	1	0
Minuteman IIIA	300	1	300
Peacekeeper MX	0	10	0
subtotal land-based	300		300
Trident C-4	0	4	0
Trident D-5/W-76	0	4	0
Trident D-5/W-88	336	4	1344
subtotal sea-based	336		1344
B-52G gravity	0	0	0
B-52G gravity	0	0	0
ALCM		0	0
B-52H ALCM	0	12	0
B-2	0	12	0
subtotal air-breathing	0		0
total U.S. forces	636		1644

No ICBMs

U.S. Forces	Launchers	Warheads @	Total Warheads
Minuteman II	0	1	0
Minuteman III	0	1	0
Minuteman IIIA	0	1	0
Peacekeeper MX	0	10	0
subtotal land-based	0		0
Trident C-4	0	4	0
Trident D-5/W-76	0	4	0
Trident D-5/W-88	336	4	1344
subtotal sea-based	336		1344
B-52G gravity	0	0	0
B-52G gravity	0	0	0

ALCM		0	0
B-52H ALCM	12	8	9
B-2	20	12	240
subtotal air-breathing	32		336
total U.S. forces	368		1680

SLBMs Only

U.S. Forces	Launchers	Warheads @	Total Warheads
Minuteman II	0	1	0
Minuteman III	0	1	0
Minuteman IIIA	0	1	0
Peacekeeper MX	0	10	0
subtotal land-based	0		0
Trident C-4	0	4	0
Trident D-5/W-76	0	4	0
Trident D-5/W-88	336	5	1680
subtotal sea-based	336		1680
B-52G gravity	0	0	0
B-52G gravity	0	0	0
ALCM		0	0
B-52H ALCM	0	12	0
B-2	0	12	0
subtotal air-breathing	0		0
total U.S. forces	336		1680

4

MISSILE DEFENSES AND
U.S.-RUSSIAN RELATIONS

Politics drives arms control as much as it does war. U.S. nuclear arms control policy moved further beyond the Cold War when President George W. Bush announced in December 2001 that the United States would withdraw officially from the ABM Treaty of 1972. The U.S. decision allowed for legal deployment of national missile defenses (NMD) of the American homeland. Russian president Vladimir Putin did not approve of the U.S. decision. But Putin refused to make the U.S. withdrawal from the treaty a reason for ceasing further arms control or future U.S.–Russian security cooperation on other issues, including terrorism.[1]

In addition, Presidents Bush and Putin signed a nuclear arms reduction agreement in Moscow on May 24, 2002, to reduce U.S.-and Russian-deployed strategic weapons by about two-thirds by 2012. The deep reductions would allow each side to maintain a maximum of 1,700 to 2,200 warheads deployed on any mix of land-based, sea-based, or airborne launchers.[2] The political trade-off for this agreement was that Russia received a formal treaty and the United States received Russian agreement that disarmed warheads would not necessarily have to be destroyed: they could be put into operational or deep storage. In addition, NATO's summit, which began in Iceland on May 14, 2002, formalized alliance approval for a new relationship with Russia: a NATO–Russia council that would permit Russia to sit with NATO's member states as an equal for making joint policy on issues such as terrorism and proliferation.[3] Thus, missile defenses were only one aspect of international politics affecting Russia's new technologies and military missions.

Offensive Arms Limitation
RUSSIA'S SHORT MENU
President Bush's withdrawal from the ABM Treaty capped a decade of

turbulence within the U.S. government and between the United States and Russia over the nature of their twenty-first-century nuclear-strategic relationship. With the end of the Cold War and the demise of the Soviet Union, the two states were no longer declared political adversaries yet still held the world's largest numbers of intercontinental-range nuclear weapons. Observation indicated that they planned to maintain their respective positions of first and second place among nuclear great powers even after reducing their offensive weapons to START III levels or lower. This distribution of ordnance and delivery vehicles might create the impression of essential equivalence in nuclear retaliatory forces, as well as of U.S.–Russian strategic nuclear equality, but any such impression must be qualified.

The Russians, because of their weak economy, cannot afford to modernize the entire range of their nuclear delivery systems. Russia's ICBMs were the makeweight of its strategic nuclear deterrent during the Cold War. Its nuclear "triad" has melted down into a ballistic missile submarine force of insubstantial station keeping and a bomber force that can be trustworthy only for regional missions. Its post–START II deterrent depends on whether its land-based missiles are survivable and lethal. Its land-based missiles are far fewer in number and less reliable in performance than their Cold War forerunners. Russia has one active line of ICBM modernization: the Topol-M (SS-27) missile, which can be deployed in mobile or silo basing. According to the program set by the Russian Security Council, production rates for the SS-27 will eventually increase to some forty to fifty missiles per year. Russia would then be able to deploy about three hundred Topol-M missiles by the end of 2008.[4]

Russia's defense ministry indicated in the mid-1990s its intent to modernize an SLBM (submarine-launched ballistic missile) and to develop and deploy a Project 955-class SSBN (ballistic missile submarine), therefore embarking a next-generation sea-based ballistic missile. The keel for the lead ship of this new class, *Yuri Dolgorukii*, was laid in 1996. However, the missile originally intended for this class of submarine failed its tests and was cancelled. Development of a different SLBM for the Project 955-class submarines was therefore required, and Russians suspended construction of the submarine until it could be redesigned to accommodate the new missile.[5] Russia will probably retain in service some Delta III, Typhoon, and Delta IV submarines. Once the first Project 955-class submarine is completed, plans call for commissioning one new submarine each year and for decommissioning older platforms. Russia's sea-based deterrent might include seven submarines with a total of 450 warheads by 2008.[6]

The turn of the century also found Russia's aging bomber fleet falling far below the threshold of minimum performance capability and even farther below the numbers of deployed platforms necessary to carry out plausible nuclear deterrent missions. On the reasonable assumption that bomber forces are less survivable than quick-firing ICBMs or location-concealed SLBMs, only about a quarter of Russia's bomber force might survive a U.S. first strike and even two-thirds might be caught at risk by an American second strike. Russian strategic aviation in 2001 deployed Tu-95 Bear H and Tu-160 Blackjack cruise missile carrying bombers. These bombers could remain in service until 2010–2015: by 2007, Russia could have 62 Bear and 15 Blackjack bombers equipped with about 550 long-range, air-launched cruise missiles (ALCMs).[7]

U.S. NUCLEAR WAR PLANS

The U.S. Single Integrated Operational Plan (SIOP) for strategic nuclear war, and presumably its Russian counterpart, were embedded in a Cold War mindset during the 1990s. SIOP-99, which entered the force on October 1, 1998, includes a variety of preplanned attack options ranging in size from major attack options (MAOs) to limited attack options, which use as few as two warheads. Adaptive options for responding to unforeseen scenarios were also created in the 1990s.[8] Under SIOP-99, Major Attack Option-1 reportedly required 1,000 to 1,200 strategic warheads against Russian nuclear forces (including ICBM silos and mobile ICBMs, submarine bases, airfields, nuclear warhead storage facilities and weapons complexes, and important nuclear command and control assets). MAO-2 adds to MAO-1 conventional forces and other military targets; MAO-3 incorporates targets included in MAO-2, plus leadership; and MAO-4 adds to MAO-3 war-supporting economic and industrial targets.[9] Weapons in preplanned major attack options are presumably targeted against Russia, China, North Korea, and a variety of geographic regions of concern to the U.S. government.[10]

U.S. and Russian strategic nuclear forces reduced to maximum deployments of 1,500 or fewer warheads would, relative to their Cold War or immediate post–Cold War counterparts, be unable to carry out some of the counterforce targeting requirements imposed by past presidential guidance. Initial deployments of 1,500 warheads are sufficient, provided survivability of at least half of the force can be assumed, to ensure that each can inflict on the other a second strike retaliation of such magnitude that their societies and economies will be turned into cinders and anarchy. Counterforce nuclear war fighting was not a thoroughly developed strategy even during the

Cold War. In the American case, at least, it was the derivative of strategy dictated by technology. A plenitude of warheads of various sizes could be made available, and a variety of platforms were capable of delivering them over polar or seaborne routes to their destinations in the Soviet Union, China, or elsewhere.

The Natural Resources Defense Council analyzed actual U.S. and Russian nuclear forces data (2001) to model a counterforce SIOP scenario with the United States inflicting considerable damage against Russian nuclear forces with about 1,300 warheads. In this particular simulation, NRDC found that such an attack destroyed most of Russia's nuclear capabilities and caused 11 million to 17 million civilian casualties, including 8 million to 12 million fatalities.[11] In a parallel simulation of U.S. countervalue attacks on Russian cities, using a minimum strategic nuclear force of 150 ICBM warheads or 192 SLBM warheads, NRDC found that a force of either size could inflict in excess of 50 million Russian casualties.[12] During the Cold War, the military argued against such minimum deterrent forces saying that they provided no counterforce-equivalent war-fighting capability and therefore were inadequate to deter the Soviet leadership who might otherwise be tempted to nuclear preemption in a crisis.[13] Those arguments are less compelling now under changed military and political conditions.

In 2006 the Center for Defense Information, a group that analyzes U.S. defense policy, reported that in the event of a Russian attack on America, most towns and cities with populations over 50,000 have been targeted, because the majority of Russian warheads (90 percent) are aimed at them. One thousand bombs exploding on one hundred cities could include nuclear winter and the end of most life on earth. There are fewer than three hundred major cities in the northern hemisphere. After major military installations, New York City is reportedly the single most important target in the Atlantic region. Russian Federation nuclear war plans have two one-megaton bombs aimed at each airport that serves New York, each major bridge, Wall Street and each oil refinery, as well as at major rail centers, power stations, and the port facilities. The Federal Emergency Management Agency estimates that New York City would be obliterated by nuclear blasts and the resulting firestorms and fallout. Millions of people would die instanly. Survivors would perish shortly thereafter from burns and exposure to radiation.

In Figure 1 and Figure 2, a nuclear force exchange model can calculate the numbers of Russian and American warheads surviving a first strike and retaliation under each set of assumptions about alertness or launch doctrine. Figure 1 summarizes the outcomes for U.S. and Russian balanced triad force structures meeting the Moscow Treaty requirements at 2,200 deployed warheads. Figure 2 provides the same information for force structures limited to 1,700 deployed warheads.

Figure 1

U.S. - Rus Bal Triad 2200

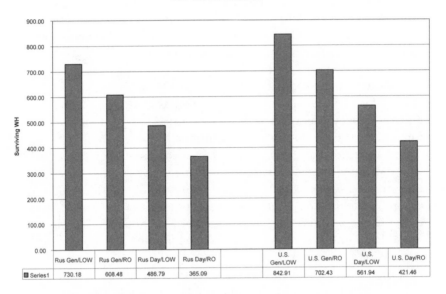

	Rus Gen/LOW	Rus Gen/RO	Rus Day/LOW	Rus Day/RO		U.S. Gen/LOW	U.S. Gen/RO	U.S. Day/LOW	U.S. Day/RO
■ Series1	730.18	608.48	486.79	365.09		842.91	702.43	561.94	421.46

Figure 2

U.S. - Rus Bal Triad 1700

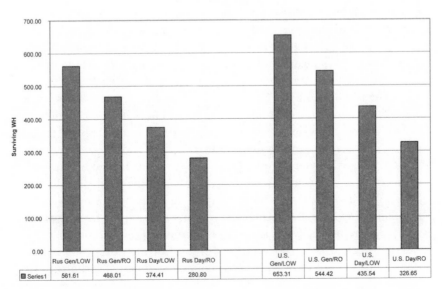

	Rus Gen/LOW	Rus Gen/RO	Rus Day/LOW	Rus Day/RO		U.S. Gen/LOW	U.S. Gen/RO	U.S. Day/LOW	U.S. Day/RO
■ Series1	561.61	468.01	374.41	280.80		653.31	544.42	435.54	326.65

Data in Figures 1 and 2 show that both states retain enough surviving warheads to guarantee assured retaliation under any of the four operational conditions. However, there are disparities between U.S. and Russian dependence on generated alert with Russia having the greater dependence. With forces limited to 1,700 initially deployed warheads, the difference between Russia's maximum and minimum of assured retaliation is alarming. The data show that Russia's forces may be placed on a hair trigger on account of this anticipated gap between minimum and maximum performances.

CONVENTIONAL AND NUCLEAR DETERRENCE
Changed geopolitics since the Cold War leads to an expectation that greatly reduced American and Russian forces should suffice for future nuclear deterrent missions. Additionally, Revolution in Military Affairs and third-wave information-driven economies have appeared. The RMA and information revolution have given an advantage to those armed forces that can adjust most rapidly to the weapons, control systems, and intelligence requirements of the postmodern era of globalized information, finance, and technology. The United States leads in this area as the first technologically postmodern military. As demonstrated in the Gulf War of 1991 and in subsequent operations in Kosovo and Afghanistan, America has left behind not only Russia but most of its European allies in the development and deployment of information-based assets for C4ISR, precision guidance, and stealth technology.

The arrival of information-based warfare makes nuclear weapons beyond those necessary for minimum deterrence superfluous in number and misleading as reassurance against surprise attack. U.S. or Russian ability to guarantee delivery of at least five hundred survivable warheads against any existing state or society should deter even the most risk-acceptant political and military leaders.

The Bill Clinton and George W. Bush administrations identified a select list of "states of concern" that could launch limited nuclear strikes against America or its allies, or their forward-deployed military forces, despite certain obliteration through retaliation. The existence of suicidal leaders cannot be ruled out, but it is a poor standard to use in designing nuclear deterrence and arms control policies, especially since leaders of these rogue states follow their own sets of rationale, however much their aspirations differ from their avatars who appear in U.S. war games and exercises. In addition, U.S. or Russian nuclear deterrence might fail to dissuade independent factions that are not swayed by cost-benefit analyses. Further, these factions are not under the control of state militaries. Terrorists disposed to use a nuclear weapon have the ability to disguise their identities and organizations as a means to avoid retaliation. As well, a nuclear retaliation against a terrorist cell might be neither politically prudent nor militarily effective. Terrorists are likely to fear detection, tracking, and identification as a means of deterrence far more than any enemy use of WMD unless the terrorists have bases, depots, and infrastructure that can be easily targeted.

The propensity of rogue states or nonstate actors to attack U.S. soil with weapons of mass destruction is probably unrelated to the size of the American nuclear arsenal above a minimum deterrent of approximately one thousand deployed and five hundred or so survivable warheads.

Whether a peer competitor will arise in Beijing or elsewhere to threaten U.S. or Russian strategic nuclear preeminence between now and mid-century is unknown—but not impossible. If so, a challenge from a peer competitor could be offset by U.S. modernization of offenses and perhaps some combination of offenses and defenses based on new physical principles. Russia's economic development is as uncertain as the future of its nuclear modernization programs. But Russia is unlikely to view with complacency a Chinese push for essential nuclear equivalence, given the two states' geographic contiguity and China's apparent desire to become an economic and military superpower. Russia currently has more expertise and experience in deploying strategic nuclear forces compared to China and has operated under variable peacetime and crisis conditions.

Given its economic disadvantage to Western Europe and North America, Russia may never be competitive in third-wave post-industrial militaries. Therefore, Russia's deterrent will require a nuclear hangover long after the United States and other major powers have opted for information-driven nonnuclear reconnaissance-strike complexes. Certainly Russia is dependent on its nuclear capabilities for deterrence of attacks for the next decade or so. But for fighting those wars around its periphery or elsewhere in which Russia chooses to engage, it will have no choice but to evolve more professional, technological, and flexible armed forces capable of rapid deployment, joint operations, and exploitation of real-time intelligence. Failure to accomplish this military evolution, relative to its neighbors or others who might pose proximate threats to Russia, leaves Russia with insufficient military capability for conventional deterrence.

For Russia to be considered by other nations as defendable, it must rely on a credible military capability without resort to nuclear first use and provide for selective expeditionary forces in its near abroad of former Soviet states. A nuclear armed Russia unable to provide a conventional deterrent would be more, not less, uneasy about NATO enlargement, U.S. oil interests in the Caspian basin, and its border relations with the PRC and the CIS states of East Central Asia. Thus, Russia's twenty-first-century military security cannot be guaranteed or even expedited by accumulating superfluous strategic nuclear weapons.

Missile Defenses and Nuclear Arms Control

The advent of long-range ballistic missiles and miniaturized nuclear warheads changed modern warfare and seemed to defy military history. It had been an article of faith among historians that, for every technological innovation, countermeasures that favored either the offense or the defense would become available. For the duration of the first nuclear age, from Hiroshima to the end of the Cold War, history apparently stood still. Antimissile defense technologies were the subject of considerable thought and investment by the U.S. and Soviet military and scientific communities for approximately four decades. Yet neither U.S. nor Soviet technology could present a cost-effective threat even to the attacks from medium- or short-range ballistic missiles until the Cold War had ended and the Soviet Union tottered on the brink of collapse. Even then, the United States adapted rather than developed an air defense technology as an antimissile defense in the form of Patriot missiles used against Iraqi SCUDS during the Gulf War of 1991.

Because U.S. nuclear strategy and policy were so often driven by technology, missile defenses were often dismissed based on the assumed superiority of offenses. Building defenses was an exercise in techno-foolishness, according to critics of antiballistic missile systems (ABM) in the 1960s or 1970s and of ballistic missile defenses (BMD) in the 1980s. Proponents of missile defenses argued that critics engaged in deficient strategic thinking and had talked themselves into technological defeatism. Advocates pointed to the apparent Soviet interest in BMD and the willingness of Moscow to deploy several variations of ground-based missile defenses as a commitment by the Politburo to a comprehensive strategy for victory in a nuclear war.

As a weapon of deterrence, missile defenses could be assigned primarily to defend cities and population or to protect the retaliatory force. However, as protection, even a few successfully landed enemy warheads could cause catastrophic damage to the defender.

Defense of the retaliatory force was more forgiving. It would be possible to allow some considerable fraction of the attacking reentry vehicles to flow through the defenses and still provide for a number of surviving and retaliating warheads adequate to accomplish the "assured destruction" mission. From this perspective, U.S. defenses could support deterrence based on offensive retaliation.

However, defending the deterrent instead of populations was possible only if deliberately limited. Defenses that were "too" competent threatened the second-strike capability of the other side. Soviet defenses that could defend their populations would therefore nullify the American deterrent based on offensive retaliation, as would equally competent U.S. defenses negate the Soviet deterrent. This model of reasoning was adopted by the mainstream U.S. arms control community and institutionalized in the SALT treaties during the Cold War. But the argument was never accepted by a number of influential military analysts, think tanks, and political conservatives who averred that it equated Soviet defenses with American defenses—a case of strategic and moral bankruptcy.

With the election of President Ronald Reagan, defense advocates saw an opportunity to reverse the terms of trade between nuclear offenses and antinuclear defenses. Thus was born Reagan's Strategic Defense Initiative (SDI) in 1983. The president's call for a research and development program leading to an eventual four-layered, comprehensive defense for the U.S. national territory was a concept far advanced of available, or foreseeable, technology. But it had the virtue of forcing the right questions onto the policy agenda. If, eventually, credible and cost-effective missile defense technology did emerge in the twenty-first century, would America deploy it, and if so, against whom, and for what? The questions remain important even in the aftermath of the Cold War and the dissolution of the Soviet Union because the nuclear age still remains.

We are now in a postmodern nuclear age in which nuclear weapons are becoming the preferred weapons of the weak instead of the strong. The twenty-first-century argument for U.S. missile defenses now rests not on the requirement for deterring or defending against a comprehensive Soviet or Russian attack: instead, the rationale put forward for defenses now is that they are needed as insurance against a rogue state or accidental launch of tens of warheads. Table 1 summarizes technology development and presumed mission focus for various generations of NMD.

Broadly speaking, the two major prerequisites for national missile defenses to become a major component of any U.S. deterrent/defense system in the twenty-first century are:

Table 1: Development of U.S. National Missile Defense

NMD Program	Mission	Defense
Phase I (1987–1989)	Enhance deterrence of Soviet first strike	Thousands of interceptors, ground and space based
Global Protection Against Limited Strikes (GPALS) (1989–1992)	Protect against accidental or unauthorized launch	Hundreds of interceptors, ground and space based
Technology Readiness (1993–1995)	Prepare technology to reduce deployment time	Ground-based system: deployment not a consideration
Deployment Readiness-"3 + 3" (1996–1999)	Protect against rogue attacks or accidental launches; prepare for deployment three years after a future decision	Tens of interceptors, ground based only
NMD Acquisition (1999–2005)	Protect against rogue attacks or accidental launches; prepare for initial deployment in 2005	Tens of interceptors, ground based only

Source: Ballistic Missile Defense Organization, *Fact Sheet* no. Jn-00-04, January 2000, 1, modified by the authors.

- A technology for missile defense emerges that is so "sweet" that it proves irresistible to military planners and policy makers; in all likelihood, this would entail a technology for boost-phase intercept of attacking ballistic missiles in their first few minutes of powered flight.
- The major nuclear powers agree to reduce the sizes of their offensive nuclear retaliatory forces to a point at which defenses become practicable; this would assume the cooperation, among others, of the United States, Russia, NATO and China.

To speed up the process of bringing technologies into development and procurement, Secretary of Defense Donald Rumsfeld announced in early January 2002 the creation of the Missile Defense Agency (formerly Ballistic Missile Defense Organization). Rumsfeld's memorandum directed the MDA, services, JCS, and other players in the defense policy process to meet four major priorities:

1. to defend the United States, deployed American forces, allies, and friends
2. to bring to fruition a ballistic missile defense system (BMDS) that uses layered defenses to intercept missiles in all phases of their flight

3. to field elements of the overall BMDS as soon as it becomes practicable to do so
4. to develop and test technologies for prompt availability when they are sufficiently ripe or when threats demand an expedited capability.[14]

How much difference would deployable national missile defenses make in U.S. or Russian calculations about deterrence stability? We interrogated our model to estimate the numbers of surviving and retaliating Russian and American warheads opposed by various levels of deployed defenses: Level 1 defenses, intercepting 20 percent of the retaliators; Level 2, intercepting 40 percent; Level 3, intercepting 60 percent; and Level 4, intercepting 80 percent of retaliators. Figures 3 and 4 summarize how many U.S. or Russian retaliating warheads would still "leak" through these various opposed defenses to strike at their intended targets.

Although it certainly makes a difference whether competent or ineffectual defenses are assumed in these exercises, even highly competent defenses (only 20 percent "leakage" or 80 percent effective) cannot repeal the vulnerability of societal assets to retaliation on a scale beyond historical precedent. Going against the most competent defenses in the model from an initially deployed force of 2,200

Figure 3

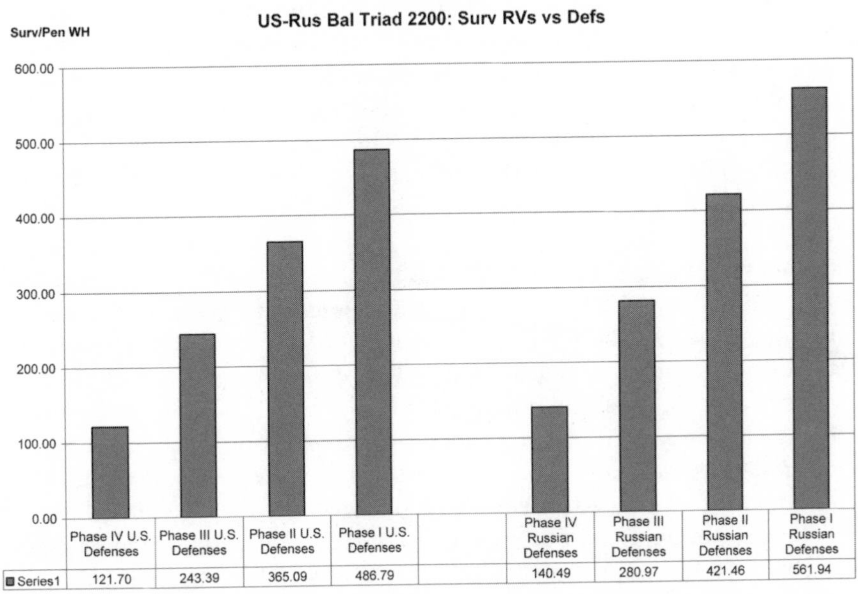

US-Rus Bal Triad 2200: Surv RVs vs Defs

Surv/Pen WH

	Phase IV U.S. Defenses	Phase III U.S. Defenses	Phase II U.S. Defenses	Phase I U.S. Defenses		Phase IV Russian Defenses	Phase III Russian Defenses	Phase II Russian Defenses	Phase I Russian Defenses
Series1	121.70	243.39	365.09	486.79		140.49	280.97	421.46	561.94

Figure 4

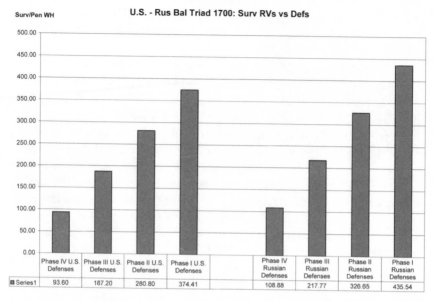

Surv/Pen WH   **U.S. - Rus Bal Triad 1700: Surv RVs vs Defs**

	Phase IV U.S. Defenses	Phase III U.S. Defenses	Phase II U.S. Defenses	Phase I U.S. Defenses		Phase IV Russian Defenses	Phase III Russian Defenses	Phase II Russian Defenses	Phase I Russian Defenses
■ Series1	93.60	187.20	280.80	374.41		108.88	217.77	326.65	435.54

or even 1,700, either side can inflict unacceptable damage to fulfill the requirements of assured retaliation. Defenses might preclude fighting a counterforce war in retaliation after having absorbed a first strike, but if two defenses were deployed then both sides would be in this mutual hostage situation. On the other hand, if either the United States or Russia could deploy a very effective defense and the other had none, then the defense-competent state would pose a possibly destabilizing threat of credible first strike followed by acceptable, as opposed to unacceptable, retaliation. This situation would invite instability and might return the Russians to the Soviets' position between 1945 and 1949.

Defenses, Proliferation, and Arms Control

The rationale for U.S. national missile defenses, as noted earlier, is no longer to provide for a comprehensive defense of the national territory against large nuclear attacks. The stated object of the Clinton and George W. Bush administrations was, and is, to develop and deploy a limited NMD system capable of intercepting small numbers of attacking warheads. The U.S. Missile Defense Agency no longer distinguishes between theater and national missile defense technologies, per se. This decision reflects the open-end character of technology development at MDA, allowing for the possibility that theater defenses may bear fruits that overlap with national missile defense systems, and vice versa. This flow model of technology development also allows for the development of NMD systems with multiple layers based on different technologies: boost phase, midcourse, and terminal intercept phases and technologies.

The possible overlap between theater and national missile defense technologies also relates to U.S. concerns about nuclear proliferation. (The issue of nuclear proliferation receives more specific and detailed consideration in chapter 6). The first relationship between U.S. national missile defenses and proliferation is the possibility that the abrogation of the ABM Treaty will lead to *vertical* proliferation. Proliferation is usually discussed as a matter of *horizontal* weapons spread: the acquisition of nuclear weapons and delivery systems by additional states. But it also has a vertical dimension, related to the success or failure of American and Russian efforts to control the size and capability of their own nuclear arsenals. The relationship between vertical and horizontal proliferation has been made clear by the public declarations of nuclear status by India and Pakistan and by the behaviors of other nonnuclear states that reportedly seek to acquire nuclear weapons. New nuclear states and suspect nuclear aspirants have made the point that the Big Five original nuclear powers (United States, Soviet Union/Russia, Britain, France, China) have failed to agree to drastic reductions in their nuclear forces despite their commitment to do so under the Non-Proliferation Treaty (NPT) renewed indefinitely in 1995.

Self-serving as this atomic finger pointing at the Big Five may be for the dissenters, it is nonetheless true that the Big Five's examples of infatuation with nuclear weapons as the sine qua non of great power status contradict the same powers' sermons on behalf of nonproliferation. Teetotalers can be forgiven for wondering why the line in front of the liquor store includes the boutique heads of state. The more practical side of this alleged hypocrisy is that, the weaker are international regimes against nuclear testing, production, development and deployment, the more fissile material is out there capable of falling into the wrong hands. So, for example, the unwillingness of the U.S. Congress to ratify the Comprehensive Test Ban (CTB) Treaty opened for signature in 1996 sets an example that creates incentives for additional states to balk at nuclear containment by means of international agreement.

Nonproliferation skeptics are nonetheless correct to point out that even the most fortunate arms control regime will not guarantee against rogue states like Iraq or possible violators like North Korea. As long as state sovereignty exists, international control regimes over nuclear weapons or anything else will have a residual dependency upon voluntary compliance by the cooperating state actors and their ruling elites. This inescapable Hobbesian dilemma causes some to argue that only missile defenses of the U.S. national territory can guard against the foreseeable possibility of a future rogue state or accidental nuclear launch. Defenses, in this view, back-up arms control with additional reassurance that U.S. state territory is not vulnerable. Therefore, American political leaders will not be amenable to nuclear coercion in time of crisis or war against aspiring regional hegemons in Southwest Asia, Northeast Asia, or elsewhere.

This concern about U.S. vulnerability to nuclear coercion by hostile regional powers is not only an anxiety about direct attacks on the U.S. homeland. It is also a concern about the potential of regional actors armed with weapons of mass destruction and ballistic missiles to deny the United States the forward deployment of its conventional military power, especially its ground and tactical air forces. The spread of ballistic missiles throughout the Middle East and Asia creates the potential for nuclear, biological, or chemical weapon strikes at the vulnerable spine of the overseas war machine instead of its claws. For example, biological or chemical weapons attacks could bypass U.S. tanks and armored personnel carriers to attack ports, airfields, supply depots, and other components of the force that are less protected than the maneuver battalions and combat aircraft. The credible threat to deny access to such sustainable support for forward deploying forces might be sufficient to increase U.S. caution and raise the perceived costs of military intervention. A wider dispersal of ballistic missiles and WMD could also place into jeopardy U.S. maritime strategy that, in the last decade or so, has moved noticeably toward the conduct of war in the littoral regions and toward the carrying out of operations from the sea against the shoreline.

These concerns about the possibly coercive effects of ballistic missiles and WMD on U.S. conventional strategy for fighting two or one and one-half "major theater wars" are realistic and are one of the probable scenarios that occupy American CINCs (commanders in chief of the unified or specified wartime commands). But it is not clear that national missile defenses are a better than improved theater missile defenses. The United States has several promising lines of development for improved theater missile defense, including

- enhanced Patriot anti-missile systems (PAC-3)
- the Army's THAAD (theater high altitude area defense)

B-52G gravity	0	0	0
B-52G gravity	0	0	0
ALCM		0	0
B-52H ALCM	9	12	108
B-2	20	12	240
subtotal air-breathing	29		348
total U.S. forces	665		1656

5

RUSSIA AND NUCLEAR PROLIFERATION: FATEFUL CHOICES AND RATIONAL DECISION

The spread of nuclear weapons, according to some prominent academic theorists and policy analysts, is more to be welcomed than to be feared. The arguments in favor of the spread of nuclear weapons have been based mostly on realist international systems theory (RIST) and rational deterrence theory (RDT). Against these arguments is a school of thought that nuclear proliferation is more to be feared than welcomed. The proliferation opponents base their assessments on organizational theory (as it applies to nuclear crisis management) and on operational constraints (as they relate to nuclear forces management).

Whether the yea-sayers or the naysayers have the better argument about nuclear weapons spread has important implications for Russian security policy, especially for the political and military relationship between the United States and Russia. If twenty-first-century Russia accepts the assumption that proliferation is benign or inevitable, then the potential for nuclear weapons spread in the Middle East and in other politically sensitive areas might increase. As well, a proliferation-acceptant Russia would maintain a large nuclear arsenal that would be available for authorized sales or illegal diversion to others. In addition, Russian support for a world of nuclear plenty is likely to accelerate U.S. interest in deploying theater and national missile defenses. Those defenses would have unpredictable consequences for Russia's nuclear deterrence and would possibly stimulate countermeasures, including Russian or Chinese offensive force modernization.

Realism and International Politics
Some theorists and policy makers now predict that the slow spread of nuclear weapons can be made compatible with future international

Table 1: Assumptions of Major Realist Theories

	Human nature realism	Defensive realism	Offensive realism
Principal cause of state competition for power	inherent lust for power by states or governments, based in human nature	structure of the international system, especially system polarity and its impact on alliance formation	structure of the international system, especially system polarity and its impact on alliance formation
Amount of power that states want	maximum power relative to other states; regional or global hegemony as states' ultimate goal	preservation of the existing balance of power and favorable, incremental adjustment of the status quo	maximum power relative to other states; regional or global hegemony as states' ultimate goal

Source: Adapted from John J. Mearsheimer, The Tragedy of Great Power Politics (New York: Norton, 2001), 22. Mearsheimer is not responsible for changes made by the author, nor for its use here.

peace and stability by mixing the same ingredients: realism and deterrence.[1] The argument rests on some basic theoretical postulates about international relations, derived from the "realist" or "neorealist" school of international political thought.[2] The realist-derived assumptions specifically relate to nuclear proliferation, and because realist principles can be explained and predicted even with high levels of abstraction, they appeal to worldly heads of state and military planners.[3] A summary of the major tenets of some of the more important schools of modern realist political theory appears in Table 1.

Proponents of international realism found that nuclear technology forced the military to acknowledge its weaknesses and convince strategists that conventional military victory, defined prior to the nuclear age as the ability to prevail over opposed forces in battle, now was permissible only well below the level of total war. Furthermore, aggressive actions that were less than total wars were risky as never before. Nuclear realists view these profound changes as directed by force and policy. They argue, however, that the new relationship strengthens rather than weakens several international relations principles. Power is still supreme but is now in the form of risk manipulation and threat of war instead of dominance on a battlefield. Peace is now guaranteed by societal loathing of the consequences of nuclear war, instead of through threat of armed forces in escalating battles.

Problems in Realist Theory

The nuclear version of international realism has a number of intellectual and policy prescriptive weaknesses. First, systems theorists are not always as careful as they ought to be in crossing over from the abstract and hypothetical-deductive logic of models into the prescriptive worlds of policy analysis and policymaking. Thus, some prominent thinkers are too willing to follow their models over the cliff. Second, in some widely cited versions of realist international systems theory (RIST hereafter), formal causes are confused with efficient causes. The hypothesized intellectual "system" transforms into a highwire player on the world stage instead of a descriptive or explanatory tool for thinking. This bait and switch from intellectual construct to Leviathan credits "systems" with behavior actually attributable to actor perceptions, goals, and capabilities. Bismarck, Metternich, and Kissinger are no longer writing the play but merely reading their lines.

INDEPENDENT OR DEPENDENT VARIABLES?

The first problem for some important RIST theorists is that, in crossing from the world of abstraction to the universe of actual policymaking, their assumptions introduce hidden biases. Assumptions that do no damage in the world of models (where all assumptions are equal, as all angels in heaven have wings) can be pathologically misguided when they leak into policy-derived explanations or predictions. For example, Kenneth Waltz explicitly compares the behaviors of states in an international system to the behavior of firms in a market. As the market forces firms into a common mode of rational decision making to survive, so, too, does the international system, according to Waltz, dictate similar constraints upon the behavior of states. The analogy, however, is wrong. The international system does not dominate its leading state actors: leading states define the parameters of the system. The international system, unlike the theoretical free market, is subsystem dominant. The "system" or composite of interactions among units is the cross product of the separate behaviors of the units.[4]

International politics is a game of oligopoly, in which the few rule the many. Because this is so, there cannot be any "system" to which the leading oligopolists, unlike the remainder of the states, are subject against their wishes. The system is driven by the preferred ends and means of its leading members on issues that are perceived as vital interests to those states or as important, although not necessarily vital.[5] Realists, especially structural realists who emphasize the number of powers and their polarities as determinants of peace and war, assume that some "system" of interactions exists independently of the states that make it up. This is a useful heuristic for theorists, but a very mistaken view of the way in which policy is actually made in international affairs. Because realists insist upon reification of the system independent of the principal actors within the system, they miss the subsystemic dominance built into the international order. Napoleon Bonaparte and Adolf Hitler, for example, saw the international order not as a system that would constrain their objectives and ambitions, but as a series of swinging doors, each awaiting a fateful, aggressive push.

If the international "system" were as determinant as systems theorists insist, Iraq would not have defied the UN Security Council in 1991, nor would Saddam Hussein have dug in his heels in Baghdad in 2002 in the face of George W. Bush's undisguised determination to bring down his government and dispatch Hussein to the nether regions. Hussein's intransigence following his invasion of Kuwait in 1991 stared down a united coalition of the world's greatest military powers, including a united NATO and most of the Arab world, and forced a UN-authorized military operation to restore the status quo ante in Kuwait. A much weaker Hussein, after more than a decade of economic strangulation, no-fly zones, and attempted diplomatic isolation, nonetheless managed to divide diplomatically the UN Security Council and NATO in 2003, forcing the United States to relent or invade with a minimum "coalition of the willing." Systems theorists might object that they cannot be expected to make point predictions about individual decisions at a particular time. But Hussein's defiance of international opinion and threats of force, as well as his willingness to go to war against enemies with overwhelming power, occurred over more than a decade of activity in international relations. During this time Hussein was the closest thing imaginable to an internationally convicted felon. Yet he stood tall in the face of systemic seismic shifts, including American military unipolarity.

Attempts by RIST theorists to circumvent some explanatory problems create others. As Robert Jervis has noted, one can divide international systems theorists according to whether the "system" is treated as an independent variable, as a dependent variable, or as both.[6] Waltz contends that the most important causes of international behavior reside in the structure of the international system, i.e., in the number of powers and in their positions relative to one another.[7] Jervis notes that Waltz's structure omits some important variables and processes that are neither at the system or actor level: for example, technology and the degree and kind of international interdependence.[8]

FORMAL OR EFFICIENT CAUSES
A second problem in RIST theories is the confusion or conflation of formal and efficient causes. System polarity is virtually identical to

system structure in many RIST arguments. But this near-identity of polarity and structure is flawed. Polarity is more the *result* of past state and nonstate actor behaviors than it is the *cause* of future behaviors. Cold War bipolarity was the result of World War II, of nuclear weapons, and of the fact that leaders perceived correctly the futility of starting World War III in Europe. Leaders' perceptions of the balance of power are an intervening variable between polarity and outcomes such as stability, including peace or war. In other words, leaders' perceptions, including their risk aversion or risk acceptance, are the *efficient* causes for international behavior; "systems" and polarity are *formal* causes.

The difference between efficient and formal causes is important for theories that purport to be empirically testable. Formal causes are proved by an abstract process that follows a deductive chain of reasoning. Efficient causes are demonstrated by observation of temporal sequences and behavioral effects. International systems theorists who emphasize the importance of structure have been more successful at proving formal than efficient causes. There is merit in doing so, and Waltz and others who have argued from this perspective deserve credit for their rigor and for the insights derived from their perspective.[9]

The danger for international systems theorists lies in transferring inferences from the realm of deductive logic to the world of policy explanation and prediction. For example, Waltz argues both that: (1) because there were only two Cold War superpowers, each had to balance against the other at virtually any point; and (2) disputes among their allies could not drag the Americans and Soviets into war because they could satisfy their deterrence requirements through internal balancing, rather than alliance aggregation.[10] The first argument is at least partly inconsistent with the second, and neither is confirmed by Cold War evidence. The Americans and Soviets sometimes conceded important disputes to one another to avoid the possibility of inadvertent war or escalation, as in the U.S. refusal to expand the ground war in Vietnam on account of expected Soviet and Chinese reactions. And allies sometimes did drag the superpowers into crisis and under credible threat of war, as the Israelis and Egyptians did in 1973.

Despite these logical problems in RIST theory, it remains influential as time passes for two reasons. First, international relations and security studies are as subject as are other fields to bandwagoning effects. Prominent ideas gather new adherents in leading graduate schools, and the products of those graduate schools carry the ideas far and wide into the profession: like St. Paul's missionary journeys in Asia Minor. Second, RIST does have one major virtue. Unlike the majority of social science theories applied to international politics and foreign policy, it is self-consciously aware of the importance of military history and of strategy. John Mearsheimer's *The Tragedy of Great Power Politics,* previously cited, is exemplary of RIST theorists ability to mine history for pertinent lessons about policy.

These "positives" about RIST might balance its negatives in a world made up of only nonnuclear powers (before World War II) or of only two nuclear superpowers (the Cold War). But an emerging landscape of "n" nuclear armed state and nonstate actors changes the context within which prior arguments worked. RIST works (conditionally) in a world of conventional deterrence, where great powers can still fight major wars at an acceptable cost. Nuclear weapons change this calculation. One might save RIST in a world of nuclear plenty by arguing that nuclear *deterrence* replaces conventional war fighting as the major stabilizing dynamic. But this argument cannot fast-forward from a bipolar nuclear world into a multipolar system for reasons that RIST theorists themselves have acknowledged: *multipolar* systems, especially those that are unbalanced, are more war prone than bipolar systems are.[11]

Spreading Missiles and Weapons of Mass Destruction

Pertinent information about the current distribution of nuclear weapons appears in Table 2.

Nations not yet appearing on this list may be more important, with regard to forecasts of deterrence stability, than those already on it. Iran is seeking a nuclear weapons capability and acquiring or developing ballistic missiles of medium and longer ranges. Iraq has been a target of the Bush administration since George W. Bush assumed office, in part because of its assumed interest in WMD of all sorts. In October 2002, the Bush administration obtained U.S. congressional authorization to use force if necessary to disarm Iraq of weapons of mass destruction and, in addition, sought UN support for a similarly tough stand against Iraqi president Saddam Hussein.

North Korea (Democratic People's Republic of Korea, DPRK) reached an agreed framework with the United States in 1994 to freeze and eventually dismantle its nuclear weapons program in return for aid from the United States, South Korea, and Japan. Leaked U.S. intelligence estimates of North Korea's actual nuclear capabilities have varied. Some intelligence community observers aver that the DPRK already has one or more warheads in storage; others say it has a limited capability to produce a few warheads of low yield if necessary. In October 2002, North Korean leaders admitted that the country had been conducting a clandestine nuclear weapons development program for the past several years and further announced an end to its

Table 2: Nuclear Proliferation: Status and Summary Indicators

Country	Strategic Nuclear Weapons (Suspected)	Non-Strategic Nuclear Weapons (Suspected)	Total Nuclear Weapons (Suspected)
China	20–30	390	410–420
France	384	80	464
India	0	70+	70+
Israel	0	200+	200+
Pakistan	0	15–25	15–25
Russia	~6,000	~4,000	~10,000
United Kingdom	185	0	185
United States	7,200	~3,300	~10,500

India and Pakistan declared themselves nuclear powers after each completed a series of tests in May 1998. India is estimated to have 60 to 80 weapons and Pakistan 15 to 25. Neither state is a member of NPT.

Israel is thought to have between 70 and 125 weapons. Israel is not a signatory of NPT.

North Korea's nuclear program is supposedly frozen under International Atomic Energy Agency (IAEA) safeguards. In 1994 Pyongyang signed the Agreed Framework with the United States, calling for North Korea to freeze and subsequently give up all parts of its nuclear weapons program. In return, the United States promised to arrange for North Korea to receive two 1,000 megawatt light-water reactors, plus annual allotments of 500,000 tons of heavy fuel oil until the first LWR is completed. Implementation of the Agreed Framework has been assigned to the Korean Peninsula Energy Development Organization (KEDO), also including South Korea, Japan, and the European Union.

Iran is a member of NPT. The United States suspects that Iran seeks a nuclear weapons program and has tried to prevent other states from providing Tehran with pertinent technology or know-how. Russia agreed in 1995 not to sell uranium enrichment technology to Iran, and China promised in 1997 to end civil nuclear cooperation with Iran.

According to UN Security Council Resolution 687, the UN Special Commission for Iraq (UNSCOM) and IAEA were to verify the complete elimination of Iraq's nuclear, chemical, and biological weapons; its ballistic missiles; and its means for producing these weapons and delivery systems. After U.S. bombing attacks on Iraq in late 1998, Iraqi head of state Saddam Hussein ejected UNSCOM from the country, and it is unclear as of this writing when, or if, inspections can resume.

Libya is a member of NPT, but the United States maintains that the regime nevertheless wants to acquire nuclear weapons.

Sources: Updated and adapted from: Center for Defense Information, *Current World Nuclear Arsenals,* http:/www.cdi.org/issues/nukef&f/database/nukestab.html, downloaded November 12, 2001, as modified by author. See also, David B. Thomson, *A Guide to the Nuclear Arms Control Treaties* (Los Alamos, NM: Los Alamos National Laboratory, LA-UR-99-31-73, July 1999), 318–319; Arms Control Association, Fact Sheet, *The State of Nuclear Proliferation* (Washington, DC: May 1998); Scott Ritter, *Endgame: Solving the Iraq Problem—Once and for All* (New York: Simon and Schuster, 1999), especially 217–24. See also, Commission to Assess the Ballistic Missile Threat to the United States (Rumsfeld Commission), *Report* (Executive Summary) (Washington, DC: July 15, 1998).

compliance with the 1994 agreement.[12] The DPRK also expelled inspectors from the International Atomic Energy Agency (IAEA) and engaged in brinkmanship with the United States throughout the winter of 2002–2003 by threatening to reprocess spent fuel rods from its plutonium separation reactor at Yongbyon. The Bush administration was divided between those who preferred a strictly diplomatic tack in defusing the Korean nuclear issue and those who advocated a tougher line that included coercive diplomacy and the possible use of force.

What can we learn from states' past behavior after the Cold War to help us infer how these, or other, future proliferators might behave?

THE CASE OF IRAQ

The U.S.-led coalition victory over Iraq to impose regime change in 2003 should not cause amnesia about pertinent lessons to be learned from prior efforts to contain Iraqi proliferation. The world was fortunate that Saddam Hussein's lagging oil revenues prompted his attack on Kuwait in 1990 instead of five years later. Iraq's massive military establishment included a multipronged strategy for acquiring nuclear weapons and a substantial chemical and biological weapons arsenal. Iraq's nuclear program was, according to authoritative sources, "massive" and "for most practical purposes fiscally unconstrained."[13] The pre–Operation Desert Storm Iraqi nuclear program was also "closer to fielding a nuclear weapon, and less vulnerable to destruction by precision bombing than Coalition air commanders and planners or U.S. intelligence specialists realized before Desert Storm."[14] Coalition target lists on January 16 included two suspected nuclear production facilities: postwar UN inspectors uncovered more than twenty sites related to Iraq's nuclear program, including sixteen described as "main facilities."[15]

In addition to the uncertainties surrounding Iraq's prewar nuclear weapons program, Saddam Hussein's mobile Scud missiles played havoc with coalition intelligence during Operation Desert Storm and threatened to cause a political crisis within the anti-Iraqi alliance. Scud attacks on Israeli cities created the possibility that Tel Aviv might retaliate, thus bringing Israel directly into the war and giving Saddam a wedge issue to divide Arab members of the U.S.-led coalition from others. According to the U.S. Air Force commissioned *Gulf War Air Power Survey,*

> Efforts by Coalition air forces to suppress Iraqi launches of SCUD missiles against Israel, Saudi Arabia, and other Persian Gulf nations during Desert Storm ran into many of the same problems evident in the case of the Iraqis' nuclear weapons program. Key portions of the target set— notably the pre-surveyed launch sites and hiding places used by the mobile launchers—were not identified before

17 January, and, even in the face of intense efforts to find and destroy them, the mobile launchers proved remarkably elusive and survivable.[16]

Soviet exercises with Scuds in Eastern Europe and Iraqi practices during the Iran–Iraq War suggested to coalition air war planners that a sufficient number of prelaunch signatures and adequate time might be available to permit attacks on mobile launchers, before they fired, by patrolling aircraft. Iraqi countermeasures disappointed these expectations: their Gulf War use of mobile Scuds compared to earlier cases reduced prelaunch setup times, avoided telltale electromagnetic emissions that gave away locations, and deployed large numbers of decoys to confuse coalition targeters.[17]

The case of Iraq is instructive for optimists about the stability of a world marked by proliferation of weapons of mass destruction and modern delivery systems. The problem facing the United States would have been different if Iraq had invaded Kuwait in 1996 instead of 1990. America in 1990 did not face an Iraqi adversary already equipped with usable nuclear weapons. For Operation Desert Storm, it had the large, forward-deployed forces built up in the Cold War years for a theater-strategic campaign against the Soviet Union and its Warsaw Pact allies. The Soviet Union under Gorbachev decided with some reluctance to support the UN authorization for the forcible expulsion from Kuwait of its former ally in Baghdad. Iraq's unwillingness to employ chemical or biological weapons against America may have been related to its expectation that a U.S. nuclear retaliation might follow to which Iraq could not respond in kind. An Iraq in 1996 possessing nuclear charges deliverable by air or missile, even over distances of several hundred kilometers, could have posed a threat against U.S. forces and its NATO allies or against regional antagonists such as Saudi Arabia and Israel.

The events of 1990 demonstrated the need for strategic and tactical intelligence pertinent to deterrence. Iraq successfully concealed from the most technically complex intelligence systems in the world the prewar location of most of the installations related to its nuclear weapons program. Iraqi mobile Scuds confounded coalition air war planners to the extent that there exists not even a solitary documented case of mobile Scud destruction by coalition fixed-wing aircraft.[18] Notably, this level of frustration marked the efforts of the winning side in a very one-sided military contest: an essentially postindustrial strategy for warfare against a static defensive strategy accompanied by political ineptitude in Baghdad of the highest order.[19] In addition, the United States and its allies had five months to build up forces, collect intelligence, and plan countermeasures against Saddam's anticipated moves, while Iraqi forces inexplicably remained in the Kuwaiti theater of operations. All these considerations point to the uniqueness of the environment surrounding Operation Desert Storm and contain tacit warnings about the potential mischief of a future Saddam, strategically tutored and more decisive.

DETERRENCE BEYOND BIPOLARITY

America's inability or unwillingness to deter Iraq's invasion of Kuwait in 1990 contains another warning about RIST optimism and proliferation. The basic maxims of deterrence learned during the Cold War years may have to be rethought, or in some cases rejected outright. Nuclear weapons and war avoidance worked together during the Cold War because U.S.–Soviet strategic nuclear bipolarity enforced a connection between basic and extended deterrence. The degree of vulnerability to coercion to be expected of U.S. allies was predictable by deducing the stability of the U.S.–Soviet relationship itself. U.S. strategic nuclear forces were coupled to the fates of European and Japanese allies who could not then be coerced into submission by the Soviets, nor by third parties allied to the Soviets, without accepting unknown risks of escalation into confrontation with the U.S. deterrent.

The collapse of bipolarity after the Cold War diminished reliable predictions about a nation's behavior on the basis of "system" variables. Former Secretary of Defense William J. Perry commented on the practical problem of nonproliferation by saying that future terrorists or rogue regimes "may not buy into our deterrence theory. Indeed, they may be madder than MAD."[20] Deterrence theory based on realist premises that assume risk averse and cost-benefit sensitive leaders may not persuade leaders armed with weapons of mass destruction and motivated by "irrational" or "illogical" objectives by at least U.S. standards. Keith B. Payne has explained:

> Assuming that deterrence will "work" because the opponent will behave sensibly is bound to be the basis for a future surprise. I do not know whether our expectations of a generically sensible opponent will next be dashed by a so-called rogue state, such as North Korea, or by another challenger. That they will be dashed, however, is near certain. As we move into the second nuclear age and confront opponents with whom we are relatively unfamiliar, assumptions of a generically sensible foe almost certainly will ensure surprises.[21]

Another reason deterrence might not work in a post–Cold War, proliferated world is that reliable and timely intelligence and warning about the intentions or capabilities of rogues with WMD and ballistic missile capabilities might not be available. According to the Rumsfeld Commission, the U.S. intelligence community had great difficulty assessing the pace and scope of North Korea's Nodong missile program and may have very little advance warning of deployment, for instance, of the intercontinental ballistic missile, Taepodong 2.[22] The commission report stated that Iran had a nuclear weapons program intended to produce nuclear weapons as soon as possible and the technical capability to demonstrate an ICBM-range ballistic missile similar to the TD-2 within five years of a decision by Iran to do so. Unfortunately, according to the Rumsfeld Commission, the United States is unlikely to know whether Iran has produced nuclear weapons "until after the fact."[23] An Iranian ballistic missile with a 10,000 kilometer range "could hold the U.S. at risk in an arc extending northeast of a line from Philadelphia, Pennsylvania, to St. Paul, Minnesota."[24] The Rumsfeld Commission concluded that the possible danger presented by short or no warning ballistic missile attacks and WMD proliferation would be high:

A new strategic environment now gives emerging ballistic missile powers the capacity, through a combination of domestic development and foreign assistance, to acquire the means to strike the U.S. within about five years of a decision to acquire such a capability (10 years in the case of Iraq). During several of those years, the U.S. might not be aware that such a decision had been made. Available alternative means of delivery can shorten the warning time of deployment nearly to zero.[25]

Although deterrence including the threat of nuclear attack may be effective in the next century, more likely is the conditional, culturally driven, and less technology oriented method. States holding weapons of mass destruction and ballistic missiles will present a mosaic of hard-to-read intentions that defy easy characterization by standard intelligence collectors. Deterrence, having been overdetermined in the Cold War, may lead the pack of underachievers before the twenty-first century is very old.

U.S. NUCLEAR POLICY AND PROLIFERATION

Decisions to lower the nuclear threshold by rogue states, nonstate actors, or other possible U.S. opponents cannot be assumed. The

Bush administration's Nuclear Posture Review, a conceptual study briefed in February 2002 that may provide a forecast of future research and planning, urged rethinking of the relationship between nuclear and conventional weapons in support of U.S. military strategy. The Pentagon study called for a "New Triad" or more diverse set of nuclear and nonnuclear capabilities for a variety of missions.[26] Components of the new triad are offensive nuclear and nonnuclear strike means; passive and active defenses, including missile defenses; and the defense-industrial infrastructure that supports offensive and defensive elements of the new triad.

This approach would integrate nuclear weapons with other military capabilities instead of necessarily treating them as separate. The new concept also implies that nuclear weapons would not be reserved for deterrent missions only, as was the case for much of the Cold War, but would be tasked with important wartime missions that were beyond the capabilities of nonnuclear munitions: for example, the destruction of enemy command bunkers deeply buried under many feet of rock and concrete. The Bush administration's nuclear policy review also calls for developing nonnuclear weapons capable of striking targets previously assigned to nuclear forces to reduce collateral damage and avoid crossing the nuclear threshold unnecessarily. U.S. military planners apparently sought a spectrum of options that would include variable-yield (dial-a-yield) or low-yield (mini-nuke) weapons so that "nuclear attack options that vary in scale, scope and purpose will complement other military capabilities."[27]

Critics of the study (portions of which remained classified) contended that the creation of low-yield nuclear bunker destroyers and other tactical nuclear weapons would return the world to the early Cold War climate of expectations. As part of its nuclear guarantee to NATO, the United States deployed numerous short- or medium-range nuclear weapons in Western Europe. Although part of NATO's deterrent mission, the weapons were also deployed for possible nuclear first use against invading Soviet motorized rifle regiments and tactical air forces. Eventually, technology development in nonnuclear strike systems and strategic rethinking, through Air-Land Battle and NATO's Follow-On Forces Attack (FOFA), improved the "firebreak" between conventional war and nuclear first use. Even so, reactions from post–Cold War Russia and China to the leaked U.S. nuclear policy guidance were highly critical. A Russian legislator opined that, since the terrorist attacks of 9/11, Americans "have somewhat lost touch with the reality in which they live." Furthermore, the director of the Institute of International Relations at Qinghua University,

People's Republic of China, said that the "Bush administration seems determined to go back toward a Cold War strategy."[28]

Conversely, members of the Bush administration claimed that their strategy was in actuality two sided. While agreeing to reduce significantly the total numbers of U.S. and Russian strategic nuclear weapons and delivery systems, they were seeking to diversify both nuclear and nonnuclear weapons to support a military strategy of long-range, precision warfare based on advanced sensors, communications, and command-control systems. Nuclear weapons were part of a new military synergy and no longer an opening to world war. It was the Bush administration's view that its critics were still locked into a Cold War mentality that treated all nuclear weapons as equally without merit regardless of their size or purpose. Whereas scholars might disagree with the assumption of single spectrum capability (including nuclear and conventional munitions), post–September 11 American policy makers seem to gravitate toward any tools that would deter or defeat state sponsors of terrorism or antisystemic nuclear proliferators, especially charter members of the "Axis of Evil" in Tehran, Baghdad, and Pyongyang.[29] The impact of Bush nuclear policy on proliferation was certain to be a subject of future academic and policy debates.

Understanding the "Other"

Rational deterrence theory (RDT)—as explained and argued by scholars and policy analysts during the Cold War—is based on the relationship between the capabilities of states and their willingness to use those capabilities to threaten. In a crisis between two nuclear armed states, each will estimate the relative costs and benefits of striking first versus waiting to be attacked before retaliating. The logic of rational deterrence theory favors waiting, as long as the defender has survivable second-strike forces, adequate warning information, and post-attack command and control of its nuclear forces. Under these conditions, in which the attacker can devise no war plan that provides for a first strike with impunity, the defender has the advantage, and deterrence is assumed to withstand the stress of crisis.

This model offers important clues as to how nuclear force structures are developed, as well as to the posturing of nuclear delivery systems and command-control in times of crisis. For example, weapons and command-control systems that are vulnerable to first strikes invite attack and are therefore assumed to be destabilizing. Survivable weapons and command systems, to the contrary, contribute to arms race and crisis stability. But RDT falls short of providing sufficient insight into human and organizational behavior that might be more important in crisis management. In addition, it is not necessarily what it seems, even in its own terms and based on its own interior logic.

The first point, that RDT falls short of accounting for the causal relationships in large organizations and small groups that make the decisions for peace or war, has been emphasized by Scott D. Sagan in studies of American and other nuclear crisis management. Sagan is especially informative on the proclivities of military organizations, including their organizational mindsets and standard operating procedures that could complicate crisis management and contribute to inadvertent nuclear war. According to Sagan, military organizations prefer preemption or preventive war, striking first if war appears to be inevitable.[30] This makes sense under many conditions of conventional warfare. But in a crisis between two nuclear armed states, a preference for first strikes becomes more of a liability than an asset: preparations for a preemptive strike or preventive war might be noticed by the adversary and trigger its own preemption. Nations that are driven toward a reciprocal fear of surprise attack experience conflict with the political objective of nuclear crisis management. Thus, the rational deterrence theory reveals its limitations when taking into account variables needed for decision making and when factoring in organizational behavior. Despite this, RDT still makes sense and its logic remains, by and large, compelling.

Rational deterrence theory is built on a truncated view of rationality. It is a rationality of means but not ends. End-rationality would also ask about the implications for society, culture, and polity—including humane values—of the various courses of action being considered for RDT and systems theory. Does the willingness to engage in a nuclear war to "save" a society or validate a policy ever make sense? Perhaps it does in a scenario-dependent manner. Deterrence theorists contend that socially unacceptable threats of nuclear retaliation are morally "good" because they "work" well enough, and they cite the Cold War as evidence. Neither the United States nor the Soviet Union fired a nuclear weapon against the other's military forces or territory despite forty-plus years of global rivalry and a number of serious political crises.

The Cold War is, however, mixed evidence for the value of nuclear deterrence as a guaranty pact for peace. The absence of large-scale war between the Soviet Union and the United States and their allied coalitions was overdetermined by politics, technology, memories of World War II, and the ability of both "superpowers" to meet most of their objectives without war. Despite these inhibiting factors, serious confrontations could have led to an outbreak of war, including nuclear war: the Cuban Missile Crisis of 1962 was merely the most publicized and obvious. The peaceful end of the Cold War was a historical anomaly to which nuclear weapons and deterrence partially contributed. The Cold War endgame was driven primarily by factors internal to the Soviet Union, especially by Gorbachev's ineffective dismantling of the old Soviet power structures and his inability to replace the old order with a durable and legitimate new system. Gorbachev desired to hold the Soviet Union together, whereas Boris Yeltsin sought to separate republics from their Soviet umbrella. Gorbachev's vision created a state of uncertainty within Russia and invoked diplomatic, as opposed to military, endgames in Germany. It was a subsystem dominant endgame with a systemic overlay, not the reverse.

Ending the Cold War rested on the willingness of both Soviet and western alliances to agree to the peaceful reunification of Germany. As late as 1989, this still appeared as a political impossibility, resisted by hard-liners in Russia and in western Europe. Against the odds it happened through the determination of Chancellor Helmut Kohl and Mikhail Gorbachev. Systems logic would have dictated a more cautious approach within the Soviet power structures, as well as between East Germany and West Germany, as less threatening to stability. The ebullient personalities of the two heads of state and their acceptance of risk under extraordinarily fluid political conditions made legitimate the repolarization of Europe. Nuclear weapons and deterrence did play a supporting role here: military adventurism by hard-liners East and West in these troubled but fruitful political times was harder to advocate or to undertake on account of the enormous American and Soviet nuclear arsenals unmistakable in the background.

The peaceful end to the Cold War, therefore, was brought about in part because of RIST and RDT. System structure and polarity did matter: the "long peace" between 1945 and 1991 cannot be explained without paying careful attention to the bipolar system that remained in place from the end of the Second World War until the end of the Soviet Union. But this bipolarity was highly conditional: it was only a bipolarity of military power for mass destruction. Cold War experience, among other things, shows how RIST and RDT offer valuable but highly contingent explanatory and predictive insights on world politics and foreign policy decision making. RIST and RDT models share parsimony with other rational choice theories as well as an explicitly defined connection between causal and dependent variables. But as related to peace and war, explanations and predictions of behavior are only as useful as their historical interpretation.

For example, from a systems theory perspective, the crisis of

July 1914 that escalated to World War I made little sense in that the great European powers aligned themselves in two tightly cohesive and antagonistic blocs rather than maintaining the flexibility of a five- or six-sided balance of power system. After almost twenty years of rivalry, mistrust, and arms escalation, many nations became intertwined in alliances that heightened (rather than relieved) their political insecurity. Thus, it made even less sense for the leading participants—especially Germany, France, and Russia—to rely on prompt mobilization and first-strike offensives as deterrents, when in fact they mainly served as provocations and as proximate causes for escalation. The "system" of great power relationships that created a tolerable and mutually beneficial stability, first forged by Bismarck in the 1880s, was deliberately put at risk by unreasonable practitioners of impractical reasoning.

The July 1914 crisis also offers cautionary tales about the validity of rational deterrence theory. National leaders in July and August 1914 should have been deterred for the reasons that the "deterrence theorist" of prewar fame Ivan Bloch argued in his prescient studies. Bloch foresaw that the military technology of the day favored defensive strategies and protracted war, which would exhaust the treasuries and manpower of the combatants. Therefore, although leaders of the great powers should have been informed, they were undeterred by the prospect of a longer and more destructive war despite the evidence of costs exceeding benefits. Instead, they invented an illusion of a future in which rapid mobilization and prompt offensives would guarantee a short, decisive war. Further, the various leaderships of the great powers in 1914 each were persuaded that they would emerge as victors in a short war.[31] Rational decision making was compromised by the intelligence assessments with which the powers were provided; in the main, these were marked by misperceptions of enemy intentions, military capabilities, national resolve, and security dilemmas as seen by the "other" side.[32]

July and August 1914 were revolutionary, not evolutionary, challenges to RIST and RDT. Neither RIST nor RDT models would have predicted the preference of leaders to risk all-consuming war rather than strategize for another decade or longer. In modern terms, the final decade of the nineteenth century and the first decade of the twentieth century were times of "complex interdependence" amid growing commercial interchange and scientific optimism of Europeans and the Euro-Atlantic region. Yet a regional crisis became the European collapse of peace into war in July and August 1914. Contrary to the expectations of Marx (a systems theorist par excellence), the edifice of pre-1914 Europe was not brought down by the objective forces of technology and intolerable social dysfunction. Instead, Europe dissolved itself by choice, and the choices were made in its chancelleries by politicians and generals who viewed their obligations to the "system" in as nihilistic a way as nineteenth-century Russia's anarchists, and they were equally determined to demonstrate that individuals with sufficient power and obtuseness could derail any system. In August 1914, not all the powers were equally dependent on mobilization as tantamount to war; Britain attempted to maintain flexibility of alignment amid the obstinacy of other powers until Germany invaded Belgium; Austria–Hungary was willing to front for German ambitions and was misperceived by both alliances as a military asset; and finally, widespread feelings of inevitable war among elites and masses in all the great powers created a besotted climate of anger and fear that propelled leaders into hasty decisions.

When these and other disclaimers have been acknowledged and the wisdom of hindsight has been conceded, the rubble of August 1914 offers little or no consolation for the proponents of RIST and RDT. Equally defiant of rational choice theory was the willingness of the powers to *continue* the war—long after the predictions of short war and decisive victory had been falsified—to the utter destruction of four empires and the economic devastation of all major combatants except the late-arriving United States. The adherence of warlords to dysfunctional plans guaranteeing only military stalemate and exhaustion, in the face of reversals in the field and discontent on the home front, also defied explanation by any theory other than policy inertia and blinkered vision.

If the future includes a collection of autocratic regimes in Asia or the Middle East as obtuse to collective security as were the European powers of 1914, and if each state is armed with nuclear forces of variable survivability with its military willing to consider nuclear first strike, if their societies are inflamed with nationalism or enthusiastic for war by religious or ethnic hatred, the potential disputants may eventually persuade themselves of the inevitability of war. If this dismal but possible future is to be avoided, it is a necessary but insufficient dissuader for the pertinent heads of state to be acquainted with systems logic or rational deterrence theory. They must, in addition, comprehend the potential of human gullibility and fallibility to overturn the system, destroy the commons, and turn rationality into political and military sewage.

Conclusion

Russia's stance toward nuclear proliferation is an important variable in determining the relative stability or instability of the early

twenty-first-century world order, compared to the Cold War or immediate post–Cold War past. A Russia tolerant of or encouraging greater
nuclear weapons spread might disestablish its own security perimeter in North and Central Asia. A nuclear arms race in the Pacific
basin would also work against Russian interests. Finally, Russia's
acceptance as a major military power beyond its borders rests almost exclusively on its large nuclear arsenal. Permitting or encouraging the spread of nuclear weapons and delivery systems in the
Middle East or in Asia empowers nonnuclear actors who may be better able to stand down Russian coercive diplomacy.

Some of the preceding points would be conceded by RIST and
RDT proponents, but RIST and RDT theorists still understate the
antisystemic potential of aspiring regional hegemons, of rogue state
leaders, and of preemptive military doctrines supported by nuclear
weapons. RIST theory offers explanatory and predictive hypotheses
that fit some worlds better than others. Two variables will help to
determine whether RIST and RDT theory will remain compelling in a
world of nuclear plenty: whether the distribution of power among
nuclear armed actors is relatively balanced or unbalanced, and
whether the aims of nuclear states are status quo or revisionist in
their attitude toward the existing distribution of international power
and other values. RIST and RDT have a lot to say about the first set
of variables but understate the importance of the second set.

6

RUSSIA'S WAR IN CHECHNYA, 1994–1996: LABORATORY AND LESSONS

The war Russia waged in Chechnya in 1994–1996 was fought with great intensity and led to military innovation and surprising outcomes. The war, defined by its scale, weapons and troops involved, as well as casualties, was one of the largest European wars since 1945, second only to the Yugoslav wars. It was also one of the largest local conflicts during the last decade of the twentieth century and the largest one on the territory of the former Soviet Union.

The First Chechen War of 1994–1996 concluded with the only Russian military defeat since the Afghan War. It was more than that: Russia's political and military credibility as a post–Cold War great power in Eurasia were called into question. The lessons of the First Chechen War are of great importance today because of the ongoing second Russian campaign in Chechnya, begun in 1999. Careful analysis of the Russian experience in Chechnya in 1994–1996 can help us to better understand the strengths and weaknesses of the Russian military. In addition, local wars and conflicts are, according to some experts, developing as "the most pressing security threat" to the civilized world.[1] Thus the analysis of Russia's wars in Chechnya may bring to light additional conditions and characteristics of future war in all of its complexity.

The Decision to Intervene and the Planning of the Campaign
The Chechen Republic declared its complete independence from Russia in November 1991, even before the formal dissolution of the Soviet Union. Moscow never recognized Chechen independence, but the post-Soviet economic and political turmoil allowed the Chechens to survive by exploiting federal economic and financial resources almost without limit and in a semi-criminal way.

The Kremlin's decision to crush Chechen independence was influenced by several interdependent factors that had developed by 1994:

- Incompetence and irresponsibility of Chechen authorities, almost total breakdown of law and order within the republic even in very loose post-Soviet terms, and large-scale human rights abuses. These realities, as well as the unresolved status of Chechnya, created the direct threat of the expansion of organized crime and terrorism beyond Chechen borders.[2]

- Increasingly violent and repressive nature of Gen. Dzhokhar Dudayev's regime, leading to large-scale domestic unrest and then to civil war in Chechnya with the prospective destabilizing impact across all Northern Caucasus.[3]

- Disastrous fiasco of anti-Dudayev forces during the November 1994 raid on Grozny, despite massive Russian support and direct involvement in military operations. This enormously damaged Moscow's prestige in its North Caucasian provinces and created the risk of a potential chain reaction of political instability and riots across the entire region.[4]

- Risk that Chechen domestic troubles could provoke the adventurous and unpredictable Dudayev to apply for support from neighboring Muslim republics and thus inflame all-Caucasian war against Moscow's rule.[5]

- Growing and widespread concern within the Russian political elite that the instability in the Caucasus and in Chechnya particularly (where the Baku-Novorossiisk pipeline lay) undermine Russia's vital strategic interests in the developing "Great Game" for Caspian oil.[6]

Thus, Moscow concluded that the Chechen crisis presented a clear danger and an urgent challenge to Russian national security and, in addition, that it had to be resolved by military force.[7] In October 1994, the Special Operational Group on Chechnya under Col. Gen. Anatoliy Kvashnin was organized within the Russian General Staff to prepare the intervention.[8] Despite well-known controversial statements from Russian top military commanders about the expected character of the operation (from overoptimistic to extremely grim), the Russian military command failed to grasp the nature of the coming war. Instead of a rapid police action against a disintegrating buccaneer republic, the Russian army had to face "the quasi-Muslim, well-armed state, led by a committed core of dedicated fighters."[9]

The creation of a Chechen military force was the only field where the Dudayev regime succeeded, thanks to the huge arsenal the Russian troops left behind when they withdrew from Chechnya in June 1992. By December 1994, General Dudayev had significant and effective military potential. The Chechen armed forces fell into three main organizational and functional categories:

The Chechen standing army (11,000–16,000 troops)
The National Guard (62,000 men)
The local self-defense forces (30,000 men)

Additionally, the Presidential Palace, the Interior Ministry, the Department of State Security, and the Civil Defense Service had their own military formations. The Chechens also had 98 tanks (T-72, T-62), 150 armored vehicles (BTR-70), and almost 300 guns and mortars. The Chechen air force had nearly 265 aircraft—three MiG-17 fighters, two MiG-15 UTIs, six An-2, as well as 119 training aircraft L-29 and L-39, and two Mi-8 helicopters—and 41 experienced pilots.[10]

Against those forces, the Russian command had assembled 23,700 troops, 80 tanks, 208 armored personnel carriers, and 182 guns and mortars.[11] The Russian command was convinced that highly decentralized Chechen formation could not stand against the regular army. To complete the full circle of classical military blunders, Russian military planners overestimated their own military potential in addition to their underestimation of that of their adversaries. The state of the Russian military was deeply affected by serious problems in the Russian economy. Its main characteristics, which influenced the combat performance of the Russian troops in Chechnya, were the following:

- Overwhelming (on the level from 35 to 40 percent) shortage of manpower and a critical deficiency of combat-ready detachments. This shortfall forced the Russian Command to rely heavily on airborne troops since they maintained the highest manning levels (almost 85 percent of full strength allotment) as well as to mix units from ground forces, marines, internal troops, and other security and police agencies all over the country. These measures aggravated significantly inter-service coordination.[12]
- A critical shortage of combat training, particularly in urban and mountainous terrain. Combat training in the air force was also deficient with its training level 60 percent below the necessary minimum.[13]
- Obsolete weaponry and equipment (about 70 percent of total material).[14] Because of the lack of material resources many tanks (T-72 and even T-80) and almost all attack helicopters entered Chechnya without effective protection

against the enemy's weapons. Additionally, all Russian combat helicopters (Mi-24, Mi-8, Mi-6) were unable to operate
and use their weapons effectively at night and in adverse
weather conditions.[15]

The use of the Russian conscript army in domestic conflict without
clearly defined political goals revitalized the "Afghan syndrome": an
unwillingness to fight. Incompetence of military commanders, particularly at the beginning of the war, and widespread corruption
dropped the morale of the troops even lower. The Russian officer
corps was in disagreement about the goals and ways of the Chechen
operation. A number of military commanders were concerned about
Russia's military unpreparedness.[16] According to Anatol Lieven some
577 officers of all ranks reportedly were disciplined, were sacked, or
left the army in protest against the war.[17]

All these ills of the Russian army overlapped during the conflict and contributed to Russian military mistakes and failures at the
beginning of the war as well as to Russia's final defeat. Bad training
of troops as well as obsolete equipment, including tools of communication, made coordination between detachments in combat extremely
complex. Additionally, the shortage of qualified personnel precluded
the use of the few precision-guided munitions that the Russian military had at its disposal, like new helicopters Ka-50, Mi-28, or precision artillery shells and missiles.

Additionally, there were numerous mistakes in planning the
operation, which contributed to Russia's debacle in Chechnya. Errors in planning and direction of the campaign in Chechnya were so
colossal that they were almost criminal. As one expert analyst noted,
"Back in late 1994, the Russian Army hardly had a clue about what
sort of war it was fighting and how it should perform, mixing up the
experience from Afghanistan with some lessons from post-Soviet
'peace' operations."[18] The failure of the planning of the Chechen war
was made possible by a number of interrelated factors. The most
important of those were:

- The Russian intelligence community, struggling with huge
  budget and personnel problems, failed to anticipate the scale
  of the conflict and the character of the combat that the
  Russian army would have to experience in Chechnya. Russian intelligence services were unable to employ effective
  special operations to decapitate the enemy leadership, following the Afghan scenario of 1979. In addition, they vastly
  underestimated the strength of the Chechen forces and

overestimated the potential of anti-Dudayev opposition in Chechnya.[19] Thus, the Russian political and military leadership was absolutely convinced that large-scale military demonstration in Chechnya would be enough to restore constitutional order in the breakaway republic.

- The military decision-making process witnessed the collapse of the routine chain of command in the Ministry of Defense and in the North Caucasian Military District. There were numerous complaints within the Russian high military command about weak preparedness of the overstretched Russian army for military adventure in Chechnya.[20] In an attempt to resolve the problem, an extremely cumbersome command structure involving several ministries was created. This command hydra aggravated the already confused coordination of services employed in the Chechen operation and military decision making on Chechnya.[21]

- The military option was dictated very much by Russian domestic politics. The strengthening influence of neo-imperialistic and nationalist elements within the Russian political elite, in addition to the growing trend to impose centralized control over Russia's rebellious regions, expedited significantly the decision to invade Chechnya.[22] The lack of a proper and clear decision-making mechanism in Russia's Caucasian policy was bad enough. It occurred within a larger scenario of President Yeltsin's struggle for survival in the mix of secrecy, corruption, and improvisation of Kremlin politics, contributing significantly to the fatal decision to launch the war. As one high-ranking official said, "We need a small victorious war to raise the President's rating" following the American example of quick and decisive intervention in Haiti.[23] In addition, the Kremlin was very much concerned about the rising influence of Ruslan Khasbulatov—Yeltsin's long term rival—within anti-Dudayev opposition.[24]

To summarize, this dangerous and self-destructive combination of politico-military incompetence, self-deception, arrogance, poor intelligence, and chaotic decision making propelled the once formidable and now degraded Russian army into Chechnya.

The Strategies of the Antagonists and the Course of the War

The Russian army in 1994 returned to the ground where it struggled with the mountainous insurgents in one of the longest wars in Russian history. In the Caucasian War of 1817–1864 the Russian strength in numbers and firepower was matched by difficult terrain and by the Chechens skillful guerrilla performance. Having learned from their initial mistakes the Russians under Gen. Aleksei Yermolov developed a strategy of siege and total warfare, which led them to final military victory.[25]

The modernized version of the "Yermolov doctrine" should have fashioned Russia's operation in Chechnya as a series of consecutive steps. These would include a prolonged air campaign intended to disrupt the enemy's communications, a limited invasion and occupation of the northern Chechen plains, and air bombardments and constant commando raids on the rebels' strongholds.[26] Instead, the Russian strategy in Chechnya evolved from a police action and military demonstration to a blitzkrieg invasion, overestimating its own abilities as well as underestimating those of the enemy. To counter the Russian strategy, the Chechen Command improvised its own approach to war, based on attrition as well as on indirect actions, surprise, and improvisation. As Lester Grau noted, "[T]he Russian war in Chechnya was planned as a rapid war of annihilation and became a bloody, protracted war of attrition."[27]

At the beginning of the war and even before the start of open hostilities, the Russian air force almost totally destroyed all Chechen airfields (including Grozny, Khankala, Kalinovskaya) and wiped out all 251 Chechen military and civil aircraft. This victory came easily. Chechens simply lacked effective air defense. For example, they did not have radar at all. Thus, at the beginning of large-scale ground operations, the Russians had complete command in the air. Some analysts mentioned that the short and effective Russian air campaign was instrumental in prevention of possible Chechen strikes on Russian territory.[28] The Russian air force also attacked Chechen strategic targets in Grozny and its vicinity. The effect of these bombing raids was diminished by unfavorable weather conditions.

On the ground the Russian troops advanced to Grozny in three axes: from Mozdok (the Northern Task Force), from Vladikavkaz (the Western Task Force), from Kizliar (the Southeastern Task Force). Russia's desire to make an impressive military demonstration while moving through population centers of border areas proved to be counterproductive: troops of the Western and Southeastern task forces were blocked and effectively slowed by civilian protests in Ingushetiya and Dagestan.

This allowed the Chechen Command to concentrate its forces against the Russian Northern Task Force. On December 13, 1995, they heavily attacked Russian armored columns near Dolinskoe village with "Grad" multiple rocket launcher systems (MRLS). In this engagement the Russians, using their advantages in organization and firepower, outmaneuvered the Chechens and managed to cross the Terek River and take Romanovskoe, Tolstoi–Yurt, and Grozny's airport Severny. The advancing Russian troops made a surprise dash from Tolstoi–Yurt to the southeastern outskirts of Grozny, capturing the second Grozny's airfield Khankala and cut off the strategic Rostov–Baku highway and the chief Chechen supply routes from Argun to Grozny.

According to some estimates, the battles for the northeastern approaches to Grozny resulted in 44 men killed (official reports) or more than 500 killed (media reports) and 150 units of weaponry destroyed on the Russian side. The Chechens declared the loss of 1,850 of their fighters and civilians and about 40 units of munitions.[29] Civilian protests and mobile defense enabled the Chechens to slow the Russian advance in order to gain time for preparation of the defense of Grozny. To the advantage of Chechen defenders, the Russians failed to seal the city completely owing to the shortage of troops.

The capture of the Chechen capital should have been the culmination of the Russian pre-planned military-police action in Chechnya. The order of the battle and preliminary intentions of the belligerents were:

- The Russians had 38,000 troops, 230 tanks, 454 armored vehicles, 338 guns and mortars. The Russian Command intended to slash the Chechen defenses by four simultaneous armor assaults from the northern, the northeastern, the eastern, and the western directions; to join its forces in the center of the city; to take the strategic objects inside the Chechen capital; and to disarm the rebels and pacify Grozny. The key task was assigned to the Northern and Western task forces: to take bridges across the Sunzha River and to seal the downtown areas. This perfectly looking "Prussian-school" plan had, nevertheless, some significant defects in the Chechens' favor. First, the Russians did not have enough infantry to support their armored columns. Second, the plan depended very much on questionable coordination between Russian units. Third, bad weather and complex urban terrain precluded close air and artillery support to the assaulting troops.[30] Fourth, the most obvious blunder of the Russian plan was its ignorance of any chances for serious Chechen resistance (for the first assault only 5,000 Russian troops were assigned).

- At the beginning of the battle the Chechens, according to some estimates, had almost 15,000 troops, 50 tanks, 100 armored vehicles, 30 "Grad", MRLS 60 guns and mortars,[31] and about 150 antiaircraft systems.[32] The Chechen Command intended to exhaust the Russian troops in fierce battles, using three consecutive lines of defense within the city. The cornerstone of the Chechen strategy was the use of the center of Grozny as the giant trap for the advancing Russians: to surround them, to concentrate at the same time Chechen forces, and to obtain tactical and operational superiority over the enemy.

The Chechen strategy, more suitable for urban warfare, succeeded. The Russian assault on New Year's Eve turned to almost complete disaster. Russian troops were able to break through the outer perimeter of the enemy's defense, but in the downtown areas the Chechens surrounded Russian tank columns with weak infantry support and smashed them almost completely, as in the case of the 131st Maikop Motor-Rifle Brigade from the Northern Task Force. The Russian Command also lost control over most of the remnants of its units besieged inside Grozny.

In desperation, the Russian Command changed the commanders of two task forces, regrouped and reinforced its troops with detachments from other military districts and from three Russian naval fleets, and entered fierce house-to-house fighting in Grozny. Under the cover of some of the heaviest and most indiscriminate bombardment in modern history, the new Russian task forces (the Southern, under Lt. Gen. Ivan Babichev, and the Northern, led by energetic Maj. Gen. Lev Rokhlin) joined forces in the center of the city. The Russian Marines hoisted the St. Andrews naval ensign on the entrance to the Presidential Palace—the center of the Chechen defense. The separatists attempted to organize the new front line along the Sunzha River, undertook fierce counterattacks, but failed. By February 3, 1995, Grozny was in the Russian hands. The battle of Grozny of January 1995 incurred casualties:

- According to Russian defense minister Pavel Grachev, Russian losses were 534 men killed. Other sources estimated from 1,146 to 1,800 troops killed and wounded, and 225 units of armor, including 62 tanks, totally destroyed.[33]
- The Chechen losses were from 2,000 to 2,500 killed, and 26 tanks, 63 guns, and 40 units of armor destroyed.[34]

It was, from the standpoint of Russian morale, a much needed military victory. Having temporarily secured Grozny, the Russians took over the political center and symbol of the Dudayev regime, gaining control over strategic passages from the mountains through the Khankala gorge into the Chechen flatlands. At the same time, the battle of Grozny gave the Chechens the opportunity to retreat in order to regroup and organize resistance in central and southern Chechnya, and most important, to prepare for a long guerrilla campaign. As General Dudayev prophesied then, "The war will be very long. In my opinion it may last fifty years."[35]

The temporary Russian occupation of Grozny did not mean the end of the war in Chechnya.[36] The battle of Grozny was only an overture to the real nature of the protracted war in Chechnya, "incredibly horrible war that they have not witnessed since the year of 1941."[37]

The Russian Command was slow to understand adequately these realities. During one Defense Ministry conference, Gen. Pavel Grachev described the operation as the "special army operation" while Gen. Anatoliy Kvashnin talked about about "real war" in Chechnya.[38] After Grozny there never was any solid Chechen front line, except in the Argun-Gudermes region, and the Russian Command over optimistically declared the end of the military phase of the operation.

The Chechens masterminded the imposition of a strategy of protracted conflict on their Russian enemies. "After initial bloody storm of Grozny," noted Anatol Lieven, "the 'modern' Russian army with its immense superiority in all the weapons needed for a decisive 'Clausevitzian' battle, usually tried to avoid such battles and proceeded by indirect and evasive means."[39]

The Russian campaign in Central Chechnya (February–June 1995) was the most successful one in the course of the entire war. Having learned the lessons of Grozny, the Russian troops tried to adapt their tactics and techniques to prolonged warfare. They kept the strategic initiative, actively and skillfully used their air and firepower superiority, relied on mobility and airborne assaults, and used infantry very cautiously in order to minimize their losses.[40]

At the beginning of their advance the Russians massed about 200,000 army troops and 18,000 interior troops in Chechnya and around it.[41] Of those troops 55,000 were engaged in active combat. The Chechen forces (7,000 to 15,000 men) had 30 tanks and 15 MRLS and consisted of two groups: the western group and the eastern group, the main one.[42] The most important operations during the campaign in Central Chechnya were as follows:

- The Argun-Gudermes-Shali Operation (March–April 1995), in which the Russian Northern Task Force suppressed and outmaneuvered the Chechens, using combined warfare (armor advance, forced crossing, and tactical airborne assaults) and gained control over the important railway and road routes in the eastern part of Chechnya.
- Shatoi-Vedeno-Bamut Operation (April–June 1995), in which the Russian Southeastern Task Force under the cover of heavy artillery barrage and air bombardment, managed to break through the Chechen defense lines, crushed the resistance of the enemy's small semi-guerrilla groups, and took over the Bamut fortress after the stubborn siege and assault.

Since the beginning of the war the Russians had lost more than 2,000 troops, and the Chechens about 12,000 men.[43] The Chechens had also lost most of their armor. Other sources estimated Russian losses by September 1995 as 1,650 troops killed and 6,263 wounded and Chechen losses at 2,230 fighters killed and 5,000 wounded. The overall human losses, including civilian ones, during the war in Chechnya were estimated as 40,000.[44]

By the end of this first successful campaign the Russians had gained control over 80 percent of Chechen territory and almost all population centers of the republic. With these results achieved, the Russian Military Command passed the chief responsibility for the campaign to the Russian interior ministry troops in Chechnya. General Dudayev still could count on support from 40,000 to 45,000 Chechen volunteers in the mountains, but because he controlled such a tiny territory, the chances for the Chechens to continue the war were perceived as rather miserable by Russian analysts.[45] Russian commentators also stressed the extreme shortage of the Chechen material resources and the unquestionable Russian control of the air over Chechnya.[46]

These early setbacks to the organized Chechen resistance pushed the Chechens to change their strategy radically. While the Chechen chief of staff Col. (later general) Aslan Maskhadov tended to continue the guerrilla campaign in the mountains, the famous warlord Shamil' Basaev chose the high-risk strategy—to take the war deeply inside other parts of Russian state territory. His terrorist raid on Budyonnovsk, the hostage crisis and dramatic standstill there from April 13–21, 1995, was the real turning point of the war. According to Mark Galeotti, the raid was the psychological "turning point, at which Moscow begins to reconsider the cost of its current operation in

Chechnya and the possible virtues in negotiations."[47] Accounts of the command-control for the Budyonnovsk operation differed. Some analysts, including those from Russian intelligence, argued that this action was coordinated with General Dudayev.[48] Shamil' Basaev himself stressed that he and his men had lost all communications with the high Chechen command by June 1995.[49] Aslan Maskhadov had learned about the raid from TV.[50]

In contrast to several earlier Russian peace initiatives, the peace talks after Budyonnovsk were imposed on the Kremlin under brutal terrorist threat. From July 1995 until December 1995 negotiations between the Russians and the Chechens, including those with participation by the Organization for Security and Cooperation in Europe (OSCE), were consistently punctuated with fighting and military operations. Both sides, the Russian army and the Chechen militants alike, viewed these talks and numerous cease-fire agreements merely as an opportunity to obtain a breaking space, in order to regroup forces, to consolidate their respective positions, and to prepare for the new round of fighting.

The Russian strategy in these new conditions was clearly defined by the defense minister, army general Pavel Grachev, "[T]he negotiations and military operations must continue hand in hand."[51] This "Grachev Doctrine" stressed the need to combine military pressure on the separatists with the search for the political solution on Russian terms and obviously was aimed at regaining the strategic initiative in the conflict. As far as the conflict proceeded the Russians found themselves deadlocked in a classical colonial war: their military posts and bases were deployed across almost all Chechnya, but their supply routes and command and communication centers were under constant strikes and ambushes by separatists. During all major military operations the Russians obtained military victories, yet they failed to establish effective control on the ground. There were a lot of towns and villages that the federal troops had to storm and occupy again and again.[52] Difficult terrain, favorable for the separatists, made it almost impossible to seal the Chechen borders completely, cut off the supply routes of the rebels, and thus isolate the theater of the war effectively.[53] Even the major Russian success—the death of General Dudayev on April 21–22, 1996, under Russian air strike—could not change the course of the conflict, despite some psychological and propaganda effect.

The military stalemate weakened the second track of Russia's Chechen policy—the pursuit of a peace settlement favorable to Russia in the troubled republic. The Kremlin ignored numerous proposals to save face by unilateral de-escalation of the conflict and withdrawal of its troops.[54] The initiative to demilitarize the conflict through a compromise solution on the basis of free elections in the republic and its membership in the Commonwealth of Independent States, proposed by some moderate Chechen politicians, failed as well.[55]

Instead, the Yeltsin government tried to impose a pro-Russian puppet regime in Chechnya. Owing to the lack of effective Russian military support this strategy failed, but it succeeded in splitting Chechen society and in transforming war-shattered Chechen politics into complete chaos. The Russian military and the civilian authorities in the republic were not successful in obtaining the real and solid Chechen popular support. They, as in the case of Russia's larger policy aims in Chechnya, were increasingly dependent on Moscow's protégés in Chechnya and their intrigues with the rival factions in Russian domestic politics on the eve of presidential elections of 1996 in Russia.

Growing instability in Chechnya and the mysterious wave of terrorist attacks against some Russian high-ranking officials in the republic in September and October 1995 canceled any hope for a negotiated solution of the conflict. The attacks were allegedly committed by the hard-liners within the Chechen resistance.[56]

The Chechen strategy in this period of the war effectively integrated military and political goals of the separatists and actively exploited Russia's difficulties. On the one hand, the Chechens successfully established themselves in the changing pattern of guerrilla war, using highly mobile operations, deadly ambushes, and surprise strikes on the enemy.[57] The guerrillas enjoyed free run on the territory outside Russian garrisons, using their freedom to strike targets when and where they had decided.[58] The Chechen attack on Gudermes, Urus-Martan, and Achkhoi-Martan in December 1995 demonstrated the Russian military's inability to control the situation in the republic. In 1996, a presidential election year, massive assault of some 1,800 separatists on Grozny from March 6 to 11 clearly damaged Moscow's prestige and influence in Chechnya.[59]

However, to capitalize on the psychological impact of dramatic shocks on the Russian public, Chechen warlord Salman Raduyev undertook another large-scale terrorist raid on Kizliar in neighboring Dagestan on January 9–18, 1996. The massive Russian operation against the terrorists and the standstill in Pervomaiskoe revealed a deep demoralization of the Russian army, including elite units.[60] While claiming the final retreat of the terrorists as a military victory, the Russian Command, nevertheless, unwillingly admitted its inability to eliminate terrorism in Chechnya.[61]

By the summer of 1996, the course of the Chechen war turned to an unstable military equilibrium of the belligerents.[62] To change it radically in their favor the Chechens needed to challenge the Russians openly and in a major conventional engagement. The final Chechen assault on Grozny was "the most daring and ambitious operation in the twenty-month war."[63] As for the order of battle, the Russians had some 7,500 interior troops inside the city and the army troops in the neighboring military bases Khankala and Severny. The whole garrison consisted of some 12,000 men.[64] The Chechens, according to Russian estimates, had the manpower potential of about 6,000.[65] The separatists designed their operation thoroughly and in close secrecy. The key to success was the ability of the rebels to strike the Russians simultaneously in all major strategic points of Chechnya in order to deny maneuverability to the enemy. The operational plan stressed high mobility by the Chechen forces, effective blockade of Russian units, and organization of deadly ambushes on possible enemy's supply routes. Most important, the Chechen plan clearly defined the political and strategic goal of the operation—to gain control over Grozny and finally demonstrate Russia's inability to win the war.[66]

Russian troops were completely surprised by the rebels' large-scale attack on major Chechen cities during August 6–16, 1996. The rebels succeeded in taking Argun and Gudermes, infiltrated Grozny, and rapidly increased their forces from an initial 500 to 2,000 men. They isolated Russian units, cut off almost all enemy supply routes, engaged Russian reinforcements in a series of ambushes, and gained control over the center of Grozny.[67] The Russian Command tried to turn the battle in its favor, employing the combined assault groups of paratroopers and infantry with armor and artillery support. Yet, they found themselves engaged again in fierce urban fighting.[68]

During the battle, the Russians lost from 265 to 500 troops killed and more than 1,000 men wounded. More than 100 tanks and armored vehicles and several helicopters were destroyed or badly damaged.[69] The Russians had achieved the open decisive battle with the enemy that they had been seeking so long: the result was almost complete disaster. Finding unacceptable the option of reinitiating the war with an exhausted army, the Russian command opted for a truce.[70] The final peace agreement was concluded on August 23, 1996, between the new secretary of the Security Council of Russia, Gen. Aleksandr Lebed (a long-term critic of the war himself), and the Chechen commander in chief, Gen. Aslan Maskhadov. According to the agreement, the Russian troops withdrew and the final political status of Chechnya was left to future negotiations. The sides agreed to conduct their future relations under the principles of international law, thus acknowledging at least temporary Chechen de facto independence.[71]

The Tactics of the War

The complex terrain of Chechnya (mountains, gorges, and numerous rivers) made its territory extremely conducive for mobile and protracted guerrilla warfare. The nature of the Russians' enemy, in its turn, had a profound influence on the tactical dimension of the war.

First, because of the violent culture and history of the Chechens as the most rebellious people in Russian/Soviet Empire and the influence of Islamic sects within the Chechen culture and society, the small-sized republic of Chechnya developed as a staunch, fearless, and merciless antagonist to the predominant Russian power. Second, the tribal traditions of the Chechens were instrumental in constructing a broad, strong, and survivable network of resistance and guerrilla warfare. Third, the cellular clan structure of the Chechen society transformed the rebel formations into decentralized and highly mobile units of devoted fighters, masters of surprise attacks, and ambushes.

All of these factors complicated the Russians' understanding of the complexity of Chechen society and led them to a fatal underestimation of the military skills and abilities of their opponents. The Chechens, conversely, knew the strengths and vulnerabilities of the Russian army well. Many of the Chechen military chiefs had been experienced officers in the former Soviet army and managed the successful transformation of the Chechen societal characteristics into tactical advantages on the battlefield. These Soviet-schooled Chechen leaders further developed their tactical advantages into a strategic preponderance in the course of the war.

The major advantage held by the Russian military in conventional warfare against Chechnya was its complete air superiority. The Russian air force (bombers Tu-22 M3, ground attack planes Su-17, Su-24, Su-25) was employed to eliminate the Chechen air force and provide air cover and close support for the advancing ground troops. Russian aviation used massive bombardments and precision strikes on mobile enemy formations and its pockets of defense.[72] Interceptors Su-27 and MiG-31 were used for patrol missions in the Chechen airspace.

Even with this advantage, Russia's effectiveness of massive employment of combat helicopters (Mi-24, Mi-8) for close support was limited owing to its obsolete navigation equipment. This problem—and the choppers' insufficient protection—allowed the

Chechens to hit and damage several helicopters, as well as a few planes, despite possessing no air defense system.[73] For transport purposes, mobility of the troops, and logistics, the Russians used heavy transport planes IL-76, An-124-100 "Ruslan," An-22, and An-12, as well as transport helicopters Mi-24.[74]

On the ground, the Russian army used the traditional armored assault and firestorm. The Chechens employed "asymmetrical" countermeasures to the clear Russian conventional superiority. In major engagements in approaches to Grozny—in Chervlennaya, Pervomaisk, and Petropavlovskaya—the Chechens employed "hit-and-run" guerrilla tactics and fire ambushes, using MLRS and placing mortars and grenade launchers on tracks and cars.[75]

The battles in Grozny and other Chechen cities from 1994 to 1996 contributed significantly to the theory and practice of modern warfare. Operations in the Russo–Chechen war of 1994–1996 reflected and further elaborated the experience of twentieth-century urban combat, especially assaults on cities during the Second World War and battles in Budapest and Port Said (1956), Jerusalem (1967), Hue (1968), Beirut (1975–1977, 1982), and Mogadishu (1993).

Chechen tactics for urban engagements developed as a series of mutually reinforcing elements:

- active exploitation of the numerous vulnerabilities of the highly centralized and hierarchical Russian military (tactical inflexibility, lack of initiative, and poor coordination between units, weak reconnaissance, and lack of training in street fighting)[76]
- movement of the center of combat from the outer perimeter to city center to make Russian superiority in armor, artillery, and airpower almost useless[77]
- organization of city defenders as small, decentralized groups, able to surprise the enemy, split its units, and surround[78]
- use of perfect knowledge of city terrain and infrastructure to set up deadly ambushes for advancing Russian columns by combining modernized World War II urban combat experience with guerrilla "hit-and-run" tactics[79]

An important Chechen tactical innovation was the urban combat group divided into small, autonomous, and mobile antiarmor squads on tracks and cars. The typical squad included a grenadier with a rocket-propelled grenade (RPG) launcher, a sniper, and a fighter with a light machine gun. During their final assault on Grozny in August

1996, the Chechens improved the structure of the antiarmor squad and developed it as one grenadier, one to two snipers, two to three riflemen, and one machine-gun operator.[80]

These squads were in close communications by portable radio transmitters and cellular phones. They effectively engaged Russian troops by hitting the first and the last vehicle in each armor column. The armor destroyers were usually positioned at ground level or on the second or third stories and in the basements of buildings, striking at the vulnerable parts of Russian T-72 and T-80 tanks and BMD-1, BMP-2, and BTR-80 troop carriers. To the Chechen advantage, the Russian armor did not have reactive protection at the beginning of the war.[81]

The Russian military's initial debacle in Grozny revealed that the Russian army was unprepared to meet these adaptive Chechen urban fighting tactics.[82] Subsequently, Russian Command introduced some tactical changes:

- additional armor protection for tanks, troop carriers, and self-propelled howitzers. Some Russian observers also stressed the urgent need for developing and deploying specialized armor for urban warfare.[83]
- abandonment of initial massive advance tactics and creation of regimental assault task forces on the battalion level with assigned tank, artillery, and mortar support.[84] In addition, for close "house-to-house" fighting, small, autonomous assault groups with strong sniper support were introduced.[85]
- improved coordination of units and detachments down to the platoon level.[86]
- close heavy artillery support for assaults provided by self-propelled howitzers and by using track-mounted antiaircraft guns and attack helicopters against enemy snipers on multi-story buildings.[87]
- assault groups assigned to the specific sectors of the city and its total blockade.[88] While this method proved to be effective in small- and medium-size Chechen towns, some western observers questioned its applicability to a modern city, such as Grozny,[89] as demonstrated through the Russians' inability to seal the Chechen capital completely during the war.

During the intense guerrilla war in Chechnya from June 1995 to July 1996, the separatists employed the effective combination of classical partisan "hit-and-run" assaults, diversions, surprise attacks, and modernized traditional Chechen tactics of forest and mountain-ous ambushes.[90] In addition, the Chechens successfully used their strong tribal traditions and clan relationships to create an effective network of constant and reliable manpower, ammunition, intelligence, communication, and logistics support for the guerrilla groups. More-over, the system of Chechen self-defense units in towns and villages closely cooperated with the guerrillas and was instrumental in keep-ing the Russians under the growing pressure of fierce battles of "semi-guerrilla war," as Aslan Maskhadov called it, in almost all population centers across Chechnya.[91]

Another combat action that the separatists, facing overwhelm-ing Russian conventional military superiority, turned to was terror-ism: large-scale hostage taking, kidnappings, bombings, and similar activities in both Chechnya and Russia. Some experts argue that in this way Chechens have made their unique contribution to the prac-tice of insurgency, introducing the so-called military terrorism or military diversion operation. Stasys Knezys and Romanus Sedlickas explained military terrorism as, "[t]he act of terrorism which is con-ducted by a military force as part of an overall military campaign or for a military purpose."[92]

Although Chechen military terrorism and insurgency increased the cost of war for the Russian military and public, some aspects of Chechen strategy are still being debated. For example: Were the strikes on medical installations in Budyonnovsk and Kizliar coordi-nated with other spheres of Chechen military activity and subordi-nated to broad strategic and operational goals? Or, were they merely spontaneous acts of anger and revenge, influenced by the increasing criminal character and brutality of ways of fighting by many Chechen warlords? For example, the Raduyev raid on Kizliar and his engage-ment with the federal forces in Pervomaiskoe in Dagestan were terri-bly counterproductive from the point of view of the separatist anti-Russian "grand strategy" of unifying neighboring Muslim republics against the Russian cause.[93]

During the counterinsurgency operations the Russian military suffered a great deal from its inflexibility, poor intelligence, and heavy reliance on stationary military garrisons (like the French in the Al-gerian War) and its inability to create an effective system of control and pacification of the population.[94] Additionally, the Russians were unable to prevent the infiltration of guerrillas into the occupied cit-ies and towns in Chechnya.

During the guerrilla war in Chechnya the Russian Command demonstrated some ability to learn from its failures and mistakes. Russian commanders introduced relatively well-trained, light infantry

units as well as special forces, capable of fighting in forest and mountainous terrain in coordination with artillery and helicopter gunships.
Also, the protection of army trucks was improved considerably in
order to decrease Russian loses from separatist ambushes and diversions.[95] At the same time, as Russian operations in Pervomaiskoe
revealed, inadequate planning and coordination as well as poor pro-
fessionalism and weak combat motivation remained among the in-
eradicable ills of the Russian counterinsurgency in Chechnya.

There were also some important features that characterized
information warfare in Chechnya:

- Combat, especially fighting in build-up areas, demonstrated
  that the Chechen tools of communication (portable radio
  transmitters and Motorola® cellular phones) proved to be
  far more effective and reliable than the Russian ones.[96]
- Both sides actively employed deception and information diversions during the war. The Chechens frequently broke into
  Russian radio communications and gave false and deadly
  orders and redirected Russian aircraft, helicopters, and artillery to fire on their own troops.[97] The Russian Command,
  in its turn, several times succeeded in using tactical and
  strategic deception (for example during victorious operation in Gudermes and Shali in March–April 1995) to outma-
  neuver the Chechen warlords.
- Negotiations, political campaigns, covert actions, and military and special operations in various combinations were
  used by the Russians and the Chechens alike to manipu-
  late decisions and actions of other side, including deceptions that provoked both sides into taking unfortunate and
  self-destructive reactions.[98]
- The Chechens, compared to Russians, made superior use of
  the means and ways of information war in psychological
  operations (PSYOPS) during the war. Timothy Thomas called
  PSYOPS "one of the most important aspects of the war in
  Chechnya."[99] The separatists established strong and influential access to the Russian mass media, using skillfully
  the chaotic and shaky nature of Russian domestic politics.[100]
  These contacts were instrumental for surprising the enemy
  with propaganda campaigns that highlighted Russian military mistakes and failures. The same media access provided
  Chechens with opportunities for disinformation attacks,
  strengthening the unwillingness of Russian public to support protracted war, demoralizing the Russian military, and

creating enormous pressure on Russia's policymakers.[101]

■ The Russian army and intelligence services were able to transform their technological superiority into at least one successful "decapitation" operation against Chechen leadership: by employing an A-50 reconnaissance aircraft and Su-25 ground attack plane to eliminate the Chechen leader Dzhokhar Dudayev. There were, nevertheless, some allegations about possible western information support in this operation.[102] To the Russians' frustration, the death of Dudayev did not lead to the decisive breakdown of the Chechen command and control system because of the highly decentralized structure of the military and political organization of the Chechen resistance. One lesson of Russia's war in Chechnya from 1994 to 1996 is that hierarchies have difficulties fighting networks even when the former kind of organization is wealthier and more heavily armed.

Conclusion: Lessons of the War

The historical significance of the First Chechen War of 1994–1996 is twofold. First, it was the first real war in which the post-Soviet Russian army tried to perform as a reliable military force in the defense of the territorial integrity of the Russian Federation—and failed. Second, the First Chechen War as a local secessionist armed conflict had much in common with other local wars of the past century, but it also had a unique character. In this way, as Timothy Thomas pointed out, "the fighting in Chechnya created another historical chapter in the annals of warfare that will merit study for decades."[103]

During the war, Russian strategy, operational art, and tactics evolved, sometimes allowing the Russians to achieve military victory over the Chechen separatists. Yet the Russian military command was unable to outplay the Chechens on their ground and in various modifications of guerrilla war and insurgency. Russian military tradition includes several examples of successful counterinsurgencies: in Poland, in the Caucasus, and in Central Asia in the nineteenth century, and in Central Asia, in the Western Ukraine, and in the Baltics in the twentieth century. Nevertheless a strong combination of Soviet-era military ills (inflexibility, lack of imagination and initiative) and current problems of the Russian military (widespread corruption, poor intelligence and coordination, incompetence and lack of public support, low morale) as well as the shortage of realistic political strategy contributed significantly to the Russian defeat. At the same time, the experience of this defeat stimulated the process of rethinking of some fundamental priorities of the Russian military and security policy.

POLITICAL AND STRATEGIC LESSONS

The character and military consequences of the First Chechen War stimulated growing attention to political, strategic, and military dimensions of small and local wars and insurgencies and conversely renewed interest in the Soviet experience in Afghanistan, as well as in the western performances in the wars in Algeria, Malaya, Vietnam, the Falklands, and Lebanon.[104]

The First Chechen War of the 1990s proved that small wars and insurgencies are the most immediate threat to Russia's security interests in the foreseeable future and the country needs to formulate its military and security policy and conduct military reform accordingly.[105] The poor planning and military blunders at the beginning of the war strengthened the traditional emphasis on the initial period of war in Russian military thought.[106] The scale of combat operations as well as poor coordination of services during the war have led Russian military theorists to the conclusion that there is an urgent need to further develop the theory and practical implications of army special operations as the way to fight secessionist wars and insurgencies.[107]

Some Russian analysts argue that the Chechen War has gone beyond the classical definition of "small-scale war" or "low intensity conflict." They say that secessionist wars, which affect vital national security interests, could involve some elements of total warfare in weapons and ways of combat employed.[108] Use of force, these analysts are convinced, should follow the "Russian edition" of the U.S. "Weinberger Doctrine" in the Reagan administration—with a clearly defined and vital national security interest at stake, strong political support at home, and a commitment to the decisive use of force to ensure total victory.

MILITARY LESSONS

The experience in Chechnya suggested that Russian military leaders should emphasize new command concepts for special military operations and for the creation of joint operational groups, comprising a mix of troops and forces from several ministries and governmental agencies with a clear chain of command.[109]

Command and control over some complex special military operations that combine counterterrorism and counterinsurgency with pacification and occasional conventional warfare should be placed under the direct supervision of the General Staff of the Russian Armed

Forces.[110] Reorganization of the combat troops involved in special operations must include strengthening the leading role of the ground forces within joint operation groups. The improvement of tactical and fire independence of combat units, with coordinated artillery, air, and helicopter support to be assigned directly to them, is also important.[111] The war in Chechnya stressed the need to create in peacetime permanent readiness formations, based on mobile combined army units that have been reinforced with artillery and armor and are able to engage quickly and decisively in local conflict.[112] The counterinsurgency experience suggested the need for special training of troops involved in fighting guerrilla wars, special armor for them, and the critical importance attached to isolation of the theater of operations.[113]

Some Russian analysts argue that the war in Chechnya has proved the great usefulness of close and massive artillery support as well as the need to diversify it (creation of "fire bases," employing fire ambushes, and "fire sieges").[114] In this connection the Russian military tried to learn from its Chechen experience as well as from the American combat actions in Korea, Vietnam, and the Persian Gulf.

Russian military writers have admitted that the Russian army lost the information and propaganda war in Chechnya from 1994 to 1996. They stressed the need to disrupt the command system in a local war as well as the potential for broad employment of nonlethal weapons.[115] The war was a testing ground for Russian armor, where tanks and armored vehicles appeared to be extremely vulnerable in urban combat. At the same time, some observers found that the use of artillery, self-propelled howitzers, and MRLS, including those employed by the Chechens, was rather effective. It is clear that development of new self-propelled howitzers has been prompted by the urban combat experience during the Chechen War.[116] The fierce battle on the streets of Grozny stressed, as well, the growing value of the antitank grenade launcher in urban combat.[117]

Some Russian military analysts contend that the major blunder in the war was the failure by the High Command to comprehend the nature of the war it was tasked to fight. This lack of comprehension proved itself in the misapplication of the country's military power and in the misuse of troops.[118] Owing to the economic crisis of the military as well as to nostalgic ambitions of nuclear superpower and global pretentions, the Russian army found itself in the war with Soviet-era weapons in poor condition and with critically undertrained, underpaid, and undermanned troops. As Ralph Peters concluded, "They were forced to use what they had, and what they had was wrong. Equipment designed for war in the European countryside, flawed tactics and grossly inadequate training and command and control led to disaster."[119]

COMPLEX WARFARE

Russia's campaigns in Chechnya in the 1990s and thus far into the twenty-first century illustrate how the present century will complexify warfare in its political aims, in its methods of combat and control, and in its post-conflict termination of hostilities. Future wars will be localized in the sense that they will not have the potential for escalation to interstate coalition wars or major theater wars, but localized conflicts will not necessarily be small wars. Wars will be fought with a la carte combinations of regular formations, special operations forces, interior troops, irregular formations and/or information operations. Psychological warfare will be directed against command systems and military formations of the enemy as well as toward the noncombatant populations in and near the war zone. The image of reckless disregard for civilian losses cannot be afforded as a political liability in the age of omnivorous television coverage and satellite transmission of images from the battlefield in real time. Finally, and perhaps most important, wars may continue long past their official termination dates, as they move from a phase of conventional or declared combat between regular formations into amorphous shapes of guerrilla warfare, terrorism, insurgency, and disruptive tactics improvised for particular situations (like suicide bombings). More than ever future war, including wars for which Russia will have to prepare and fight, will be Wars of the Shape Shifters.

7

CONCLUSION

Russia faces a postmodern world in the twenty-first century. That world will challenge Russia along at least three dimensions—political, military-technical, and sociological-cultural—to develop policies and strategies that fulfill the requirements of postmodern deterrence and defense missions.

At the political level, Russia will find a "multiplex" or "uni-multipolar" world that offers a geostrategic picture of great complexity. Unlike in the late modern or Cold War era, there is no self-evident, singular source of threat to Russian state security. Threats are numerous, of indeterminate sources, and ambiguous. Threat assessment is clouded by new international polarization among the leading military and economic powers and made more difficulty by porous borders and internationalization of domestic security threats (such as organized crime and terrorism). Intelligence tasking becomes more demanding because the "enemy" or "threat" is everywhere at once: possibilities are endless, but what is imminent?

Thomas Hobbes was part of the Cold War international system, but that system had a high level of predictability and built-in stabilizers: bipolarity and nuclear weapons. Now one of the stabilizers is gone, and the spread of nuclear weapons among revisionist actors threatens to turn them and other weapons of mass destruction (WMD) into destabilizing forces. Hobbes's latent security dilemma is that Russian intelligence must transition from an era that emphasized information scarcity and secrets to an era of information abundance and relative openness. Open sources must be exploited along with clandestine collection, and the recipients of that intelligence are more diverse than governments and their militaries. Intelligence collection and analysis are now related to the demands of the information age, and that includes information warfare among businesses, cartels, and mafias, as well as governments.

At the military-technical level, Russia must engage in a higher level of RMA or cease to identify itself as a major power. RMA means more than developing smart weapons and command-control systems, although that is certainly implied. More important, it means that Russia must renounce much of the bloody-minded absolutism of its tsarist and communist past. It must also move beyond the faux economic modernization of the Yeltsin era and the kleptocracy that Yeltsin passed along to Putin. Without an information-driven economy and a democratic framework of law that supports such an economy, Russia is destined for lower authority in the international ranking of states.

Russia cannot afford to modernize its economy in order to transform its military without discarding its state-dependent military-industrial complex and without reformatting its industrial-age military organization. The Russian army of today suffers from a bewildering combination of authoritarianism, politicization, corruption, and lack of consistent political direction.[1] Russia has not experienced a military establishment in this condition since the time between the Russo–Japanese War and the outbreak of World War I. Regardless of almost certain resistance from career officers and their supportive politicians, Russia must again undertake military reform because the alternative is decay and military obsolescence, which is not a hopeful prognosis when Russia's frontiers need to be defended. Without military reform that is supported by a strong economy, the military encirclement of Russia becomes a near certainty instead of a hypothesis.

In addition to the geopolitical and technological challenges facing Russia's deterrence and defense capabilities, a third set of challenges arises from sociological and cultural factors. Russia's society was weakened in the 1990s along with its economy and polity.[2] Privatization and economic "shock therapy" increased the gap between the privileged and the disadvantaged and led to the latter's political resentment and social resignation. The winners from economic globalization and elite kleptocracy flaunted their new wealth as pensioners and displaced workers fell further beneath the safety net. Government inability to guarantee income security to many citizens created favorable nostalgia for the communist era. Parties of the political right and left drew sustenance from the inertia and ambivalence of the Yeltsin presidential party and the Duma. The public health system imploded, directly affecting military readiness and civilian worker productivity. At the same time, a global communications network offered daily reminders to Russians that their society was deteriorating even as the societies of former East European allies were improving. Nationalism and religion fueled civil war in Chechnya: old scores from the days of Imperial and Soviet Russia remained to be settled.

Russia entered the twenty-first century with a society not unlike Europe's at the turn of the nineteenth century: one based on false premises, promises, and posturing. The newly empowered rich lived well and in pursuit of a life of leisure, mostly out of the country where their laundered money was stored. Russia's political parties were personal, not popular, and promoted no serious strategies for group interests and aggregation. The Russian parliament was part of the problem, not part of the solution. Although Putin's decision-making process operates with a great deal more tidiness than Yeltsin's, it is not clear that society's major dysfunctions have been dented. The Russian armed forces certainly show little evidence of change. Underpaid or unpaid personnel, brutal hazing of new recruits, corruption, and mendacity of officers, as well as systematic leakage of equipment into black markets were standard practices throughout the 1990s. From 1994 through 1996, a Russian army with insufficient resources, poor tactics, inept leadership, and no soul force was fought to a standstill by Chechen rebels who repeatedly embarrassed the Yeltsin clique with improbable victories.

The United States faces, as does Russia, a world of uncertain geopolitical alignment combined with racing globalization and primordial wars within and across state boundaries. Despite its considerable assets, the United States has a questionable guaranty of favorable alliances or international sympathy for global power projection. For example: the first comprehensive Gallup Poll of public opinion in Arab and Islamic countries since 9/11 showed that large majorities in some of those states, including respondents in Saudi Arabia and Pakistan, had an overall negative view of U.S. policy.[3] Many of those polled refused to believe that any Arabs could have been involved in the terrorist attacks. America, notwithstanding its singular economic and military superpower status, was encountering considerable resistance to its message on the need for aggressive global counterterrorism. Respondents frequently described the United States as arrogant, overbearing, imperial, and exploitive and resented U.S. political and cultural influence in their regions.

Granted that the United States faces a complex world of multiple threats and challenges to security, the Russian pathway to success is steeper than the American one, and while U.S. public policy issues have largely been resolved, they continue to bedevil Russia. These include the establishment of a democratically accountable polity, a truly market-driven economy, a free press, and stable and legitimate civil-military relations. All of this, in the American case, also takes place within a framework of civil and criminal law that is subjected to legislative and judicial oversight. Russia is far from having attained these markers of democratic accountability or of market-based pluralism.

But Russia must be judged against its own history, which is dominated by absolutism and autocracy. It will take several generations to wring out of the Russian psyche the habits of autocratic obedience or, its antithesis, antiautocratic resistance and cynicism. Meanwhile, what of Russia's armed forces within an evolving state? Table 1 offers one retrospective and prospective assessment of Russia's military. It is based on the model developed by Charles Moskos and here excerpts five important variables—perceived threat, force structure, major mission definition, dominant military professional, and public attitudes toward the military. Each variable is coded with an assessment of the Russian military in the modern, late modern, and postmodern eras.

Table 1: Russian and Soviet Armed Forces in Three Eras

	Modern (1900–1945)	Late Modern (1945–1990)	Postmodern (1990–)
Perceived threat	Enemy invasion	Nuclear war	NATO enlargement/ Border incursions/ Sub-state violence and terrorism
Force structure	Mass army, conscription	Mass army, conscription	Mixed conscript-contract force
Major mission definition	Defense of homeland	Conventional war in Europe or Asia/ Nuclear deterrence	Counterinsurgency and counterterror/ Nuclear deterrence/ Contiguous force projection
Dominant military professional	Combat leader	Manager-bureaucrat or military technologist	Undetermined: contention among manager-bureaucrat and warrior ethos
Public attitude to military	Supportive	Supportive until the latter 1980s	Ambivalent

Source: Based on Charles C. Moskos, "Toward a Postmodern Military: The United States as a Paradigm," Ch. 2 in Moskos, John Allen Williams, and David R. Segal, eds., *The Postmodern Military: Armed Forces after the Cold War* (New York: Oxford University Press, 2000), 14–31, citation from table, 15. We have omitted some of Moskos's original variables for his framework for analysis: he bears no responsibility for its application here.

PERCEIVED THREAT

During the modern period from 1900 to 1945, Russia and the Soviet Union were faced with threats of invasion. Germany was the most obvious source of the threat for Imperial Russia and for the Soviet Union. But, especially after the Russo–Japanese War, Japan loomed large as a possible adversary for Russia and for the USSR until 1945. China posed a less imminent threat to Imperial Russia and to the Soviet Union during the modern period on account of China's internal struggles and its war against Japan. Although the major perceived threat for Russia and the Soviets was one of invasion of the homeland, neither performed admirably in intelligence assessment or in military readiness. Imperial Russia handled balance of power and alliance relationships poorly, and its skills in crisis management were found wanting during the crisis of July and August 1914. The Soviet Union's leaders sought to conciliate an implacable Germany between 1939 and 1941 but during this interval took insufficient measures to prepare for an invasion that was preceded by numerous intelligence warnings from foreign and domestic sources.

During the late modern or Cold War years from 1945 to 1990, the Soviet Union had little to fear in terms of any large-scale conventional attack on its homeland. Expansion of its pre-World War II boundaries provided a security glacis in East Central Europe that buffered Ukraine and Byelorussia from any repetition of Operation Barbarossa. Once the Soviet Union acquired a diverse and survivable arsenal of strategic nuclear weapons, its frontiers and its heartland were truly impregnable. The nuclear weapons in the hands of American and allied NATO adversaries became Moscow's major military concern. U.S. and allied nuclear weapons could be used in retaliation for a Soviet nuclear attack, as well as to deter a Soviet conventional attack on western Europe. Even a short war between NATO and the Soviet-dominated Warsaw Pact states would pose an imminent risk of escalation into global nuclear war, given the numbers of NATO tactical and theater nuclear forces deployed in harm's way. Soviet Cold War military planners did worry about a U.S. preemptive nuclear attack or an American interest in a preventive nuclear war at various times, and vice versa for U.S. leaders. But especially after the Cuban Missile Crisis, U.S. and Soviet political leaders sought to control the risk of nuclear first use, particularly inadvertent or accidental use that could spill over into a larger conflict.

In the postmodern period for post-Soviet Russia, lack of politically hostile relations with the United States and NATO would seemingly reassure Russia against fears of attack from the West. This is largely true, except Russia is wary of NATO enlargement. Russia feels somewhat betrayed over the fact that NATO had given a tacit "no enlargement" pledge in return for former Soviet president Mikhail Gorbachev's willingness to end the Cold War peaceably. Another reason is that NATO expansion to the east removes the buffer zone that formerly protected western Russia. Coupled with this, in the aftermath of Soviet collapse, Ukraine, Belarus, and the Baltic states are now legally independent of Russian control. But postmodern Russia's major security concerns do not lie to its west: indeed, rapprochement with NATO and integration with the economies of the European Union are two pillars of the foreign policy of Russian president Vladimir Putin. Instead, Russia's most important security problems are posed by political turbulence in its near abroad and within Russia itself. In the 1990s the hallmark case was the rebellion against Russian rule in Chechnya—an old story going back centuries, now returning with an atavistic flavor in a postmodern setting. Russia was fought to a draw in 1994–1996 by Chechens and opted for another round that began in 1999. Russia hopes that the United States will sign onto the Kremlin's version of global antiterrorism that includes ostracizing Chechen supporters of al Qaeda, in Russia and in former Soviet Georgia. Apart from fractious borders and internal wars, Russia is threatened by a stagnant economy and a state lacking in legality and puissance.

FORCE STRUCTURE
The force structure of the Imperial Russian and Soviet armies in the modern era (1900–1945) was based on a mass army and conscription. The peasant masses of the Imperial Russian army and the conscripts of the Soviet armed forces, however, were led by officers who were the products of very different military traditions. The military High Command of the tsar's armies included individuals who reached high status as a result of court politics and military intrigues. The serious study of modern war was not a necessary condition for advancement. Cronyism guaranteed pride of place to relatives and favorites of the tsar. Cabinet officers appointed to supervise the military were often deficient in their understanding of modern military art. Additionally, Soviet armed forces grew out of the shattering experiences of the Bolshevik revolution, World War I, and the civil war that followed. Great debates on the kind of army the USSR should have rocked the Soviet High Command and political leadership in the 1920s. By the 1930s Stalin had consolidated his hold over the commissars and warlords and the issue of a mass conscript army— led by officers with professional training and party loyalty—was settled. Unfortunately, politicized officer corps and Stalin's paranoia about Red Napoleons in the ranks created considerable turbulence

in the various disciplines related to battlespace (defined by the U.S. acronym C4ISR). Military manager-bureaucrats able to operate successfully in a market economy would also be in demand in a modernized, postindustrial version of a Russian military. The role of combat leaders would be redefined for counterinsurgency and counterterror missions and for a variety of peacekeeping and peace enforcement operations, the question remains whether that role could be professionally distinct from the politically engaged officer in evolving civil-military relations.

PUBLIC ATTITUDE TOWARD THE MILITARY

For the armies of former Imperial Russia, public opinion is tied closely to the stratified nature of society. An essentially authoritarian political system faced disaffection among its upper- and middle-class intelligentsia, in addition to a radicalized sector that favored anarchy or the entire overthrow of the tsarist order (or both). Disaffected intellectuals and bourgeoisie improved their political organization and recruitment toward the end of the nineteenth century. When Russia suffered humiliating military reversals during the Russo–Japanese War of 1904–1905, diminished confidence in tsarist policy opened the door to institutional reform within a basically autocratic framework. The tsar despised the legislature with which he was forced to work and consequently shared no information on matters of war planning and threat assessment. The modest degree of *glasnost* between 1905 and 1914 had further encouraged opponents of the regime, which escalated when Tsar Nicholas and his generals demonstrated their inept wartime leadership. The tsar abdicated in early 1917 and was followed by a liberal-constitutionalist order that did not withstand the pressures of war, economic collapse, and revolution. The final blow in Petrograd in November was caused by worker and soldier commoners asserting allegiance to Lenin's waiting conspirators. Public opinion had transformed from massive acquiescence to antimilitary skepticism to armed revolt.

In the Soviet Union of the pre- and post–World War II years, there was only an official public opinion according to the dictates of the party and state regime. The party leaders represented the working class who were destined to rule Russia and then the world (once Leon Trotsky had been exiled in 1929 and other subsequent events took place). Party ideology held that "opinions" were the product of a collective wisdom of the workers and peasants as expressed through the party leadership, although Soviet armed forces were not immune to popular perceptions that influenced policy, and for several decades after World War II, the Red Army maintained its social prestige and occupational appeal on the strength of its great victory in 1945. In the 1970s and 1980s, however, it became apparent that the cost of military preparedness was choking the country's economy, and Soviet citizens were frustrated by their lack of consumer goods and by the inflexibility of government bureaucracies. Well before Gorbachev officially acknowledged the debility of the state's political and economic orders, the Brezhnev era was all but officially acknowledged as a period of "stagnation" even prior to Soviet collapse. The Soviet army probably maintained as much prestige as it could under the circumstances, but it was a creation of the party-state with a shared fate running in parallel to it. The Soviet invasion of Afghanistan and its unfavorable international response removed the veil of invincibility from the Soviet armed forces that they had claimed since World War II. Along with the party and state leaderships and security services, the reputation and credibility of the Soviet military fell with Gorbachev and the coup plotters of August 1991.

Russia's armed forces of today lack popular respect and prestige. In part, this is because of Russia's retrenched political and military position among world powers. Except for nuclear weapons, Russia is now a regional power instead of a global force. In addition, the experience of serving in the Russian armed forces in the 1990s for enlisted personnel was simply hellish and barbaric. Russian military personnel became dangerously politicized in the 1990s by age, partisan affiliations, and personal cliques, among others. Demoralized officers and enlisted also suffered the competitive anarchy of Yeltsin's patronage-driven security establishment.

Even after Vladimir Putin became president, Russia's military and security organizations vied for political power and economic support. One expert on the Russian armed forces and security policies noted in 2005,

> No standardized basis for national security policymaking or democratic control exists: there is no parliamentary accountability over all of Russia's competing multiple militaries, no guarantee of the rights of soldiers and officers, and no executive accountability to the Parliament and the Duma's prerogative to monitor the defense budget of and policy implementation within Russia's multiple militaries.[4]

Russia's disastrous experience in Chechnya from 1994 to 1996 delivered a blow to the image of its armed forces that it may take decades to recover from, even if the rebellious province is success-fully pacified in later phases of that eternal conflict. Although Russian experience in Chechnya after 1999 improved on the dismal perfor-mance of 1994 to 1996, pessimistic estimates of Russian military leadership commend themselves to careful observers even during Putin's second term in office:

> The fighting in Chechnya also exhibits the central government's incompetent military leadership; disorga-nized and uncoordinated command structure; poorly-trained, demoralized, and corrupt soldiers; and outdated equipment.[5]

As president, Putin, compared with Yeltsin, has imposed more discipline on the military and security establishments. But leaders in the Defense Ministry and the General Staff remain wary of the growing influence of former Soviet and Russian intelligence officers who have risen under Putin to influential roles in defense and secu-rity policy. Furthermore, rivalry between the Defense Ministry and the General Staff on issues of military policy and doctrine was cus-tomary under Yeltsin and has carried over into the Putin era.[6]

Russia's dilemma is this: to the extent that it truly evolves toward a market economy and a political democracy, maintaining public opinion that is favorable to military service and to the role of armed forces in society is a necessary condition for military effec-tiveness. This was not true prior to 1991: the general public was not a force in the decision-making process of authoritarian regimes. Now, however, if Russia is to command a place on the European or Asiatic stage, it must embrace free markets and democracy and the kind of military that is compatible with both. Of course, for cultural and historic reasons, the Russian versions of democracy and a market economy will differ considerably from those of America, Britain, or Germany. Russia cannot backslide politically into authoritarianism of the kind that ruled from Peter the Great to Mikhail Gorbachev, the last commissar. If it does, it will have a hollow and obsolete military and its eleven time zones will advertise its weakness and vulnerabil-ity instead of its power and potential.

NOTES

Introduction

1. This is easier said than accomplished. For assessments of Russia's difficulties in this regard, see Pavel K. Baev, "The Trajectory of the Russian Military: Downsizing, Degeneration, and Defeat," 43–72, and Alexei G. Arbatov, "Military Reform: From Crisis to Stagnation," 95–119, especially 116–119, both in Steven E. Miller and Dmitri V. Trenin, eds., *The Russian Military: Power and Policy* (Cambridge, MA: MIT Press, 2004).

2. Stephen J. Blank, "Potemkin's Treadmill: Russian Military Modernization," in Ashley J. Tellis and Michael Wills, eds., *Strategic Asia 2005–06: Military Modernization in an Era of Uncertainty* (Washington, DC: National Bureau of Asian Research, 2005), 175–205, citation p. 195.

Chapter 1: The Ghost of Barbarossa: Avoiding Surprise Attack

1. S. P. Ivanov, *Nachal'nyy period voyny: po opytu pervykh kampaniy I operatsiy vtoroy mirovoy voyny* [The Initial Period of War: On the Experience of the First Campaigns of the Second World War] (Moscow: Voenizdat, 1974). For comparison with Russian World War I experience, see I. I. Rostunov, ed., *Istoriya Pervoy Mirovoy Voyny 1914–1918, Vol. I* [History of the First World War] (Moscow: 'Nauka,' 1975), ch. 3–4. The Soviet *Voyenno istorichesky zhurnal* [Military–Historical Journal] covered this topic extensively. See, for example, A. I. Yevseev, "0 nekotorykh tendentsiyakh izmenii soderzhaniya i kharaktera nachal'nogo perioda voyny" [On Certain Tendencies in the Changing Content and Character of the Initial Period of War], *Voyenno istoricheskiy zhurnal,* no. 11 (November 1985), 10–20. See also A. A. Grechko, et al., *Istoriya vtoroy mirovoy voyny, 1939–1945* (Moscow: Voenizdat, 1974), vol. 2, 74–182 and passim, for a discussion of Soviet military doctrine from 1936 to 1939. For an appraisal of Soviet threat assessment between the two world wars, see John Erickson, "Threat Identification and Strategic Appraisal by the Soviet Union, 1930–41," ch. 13, in Ernest R. May, ed., *Knowing One's Enemies: Intelligence Assessment before the Two World Wars* (Princeton, NJ: Princeton University Press, 1984), 375–424.

2. For overviews of this issue, see David M. Glantz, "The Red Army in 1941," 1–37 and Jacob W. Kipp, "Soviet War Planning," 40–54, in Glantz, ed., *The Initial Period of War on the Eastern Front, 22 June– August 1941* (London: Frank Cass, 1993); Richard H. Phillips, *Soviet Military Debate on the Initial Period of War: Characteristics and Implications* (Cambridge,

MA: Center for International Studies, MIT, November 1989); and Jacob W. Kipp, *Barbarossa, Soviet Covering Forces and the Initial Period of War: Military History and Air Land Battle* (Ft. Leavenworth, KS: Soviet Army Studies Office, undated).

3. According to Soviet historical analysis of the Great Patriotic War, during its early and middle stages Soviet forces were forced to fight on the strategic defensive or to limit their strategic offensive operations to counterattacks on the main sectors. In the third period of the war (essentially 1944–1945), when Soviet forces had the initiative and necessary force groupings, an offensive began with several strategic operations conducted successively on different sectors. The scale of strategic operations increased accordingly. See B. V. Panov, V. N. Kiselev, I. I. Kartavtsev, et al., *Istoriya voyennogo iskusstva* [The History of Military Art] (Moscow: Voyenizdat, 1984), ch. 10; and David M. Glantz, *Deep Attack: The Soviet Conduct of Operational Maneuver* (Fort Leavenworth, KS: Soviet Army Studies Office, April 1987).

4. Levels of military art (strategy, operational art, and tactics) are defined according to the type of campaign, battle, or engagement in which forces are used; according to the level of command responsibility for the military action; and according to the military geographical level at which the fighting takes place. For a discussion, see Christopher Donnelly, *Red Banner: The Soviet Military System in Peace and War* (Coulsdon, Surrey: Jane's Information Group, 1988), 213–214. On the impact of nuclear weapons on Soviet military thought, see David Holloway, *The Soviet Union and the Arms Race* (New Haven, CT: Yale University Press, 1983), chs. 2–3.

5. M. M. Kir'yan, "Nachal'nyy period Velikoy Otechestvennoy voyny" [The Initial Period of the Great Patriotic War], *Voyenno istoricheskiy zhurnal,* no. 6 (June 1988), 11–17.

6. M. Cherednichenko, "0 nachal'nom periode Velikoy Otechestvennoy voyny" [On the Initial Period of the Great Patriotic War], *Voyenno istoricheskiy zhurnal,* no. 4 (1961), 28–35.

7. Ibid., 29.

8. Kir'yan, "Nachal'nyy period Velikoy Otechestvennoy voyny," 13.

9. A. M. Nekrich, *1941 22 Iyunya* [June 22, 1941] (Moscow: 'Nauka,' 1965), in Vladimir Petrov, ed., *June 22 1941: Soviet Historians and the German Invasion* (Columbia, SC: University of South Carolina Press, 1968), 24–245. This source also contains excerpts from debates among Soviet military historians about the responsibility for Barbarossa.

10. John Erickson, *The Soviet High Command. A Military-Political History, 1918–41* (New York: St. Martin's Press, 1962), 447–509.

11. David M. Glantz, *Soviet Operational Art and Tactics in the 1930s* (Ft. Leavenworth, KS: Soviet Army Studies Office, 1990).

12. V. Matsulenko, "Nekotoryye vyvody iz opyta nachal'nogo perioda Velikoy Otechestvennoy voyny" [Certain Conclusions from the Experience of the Initial Period of the Great Patriotic War], *Voyenno istoricheskiy zhurnal,* no. 3 (1984), 35–43. On Soviet failures to respond to warning, see Nekrich, *22 Iyunya 1941*; and Barton Whaley, *Codeword BARBAROSSA* (Cambridge, MA: MIT Press, 1973), chs. 3–5.

13. Matsulenko, "Nekotoryye vyvody iz opyta nachal'nogo perioda Velikoy Otechestvennoy voyny."

14. On this, see Erickson, "Threat Assessment," in May, ed., *Knowing One's Enemies;* and Whaley, *Barbarossa,* passim.

15. P. T. Kunitskiy, "Vosstanovleniye prorvannogo stratigecheskogo fronta oborony v 1941 gody" [Restoration of the Disrupted Strategic Front in 1941], *Voyenno istoricheskiy zhurnal,* no. 7 (1988), 52–60, this citation on page 23.
16. Ibid.
17. Ibid., 54.
18. Ibid., 56.
19. Ibid., 57.
20. Ibid.
21. Ibid.
22. Ibid., 57–58. See also Albert Seaton, *The Battle for Moscow 1941–1942* (New York: Stein and Day, 1971).
23. Kunitsky, "Vosstanovleniye provannogo strategicheskogo fronta oborony v 1941 gody," passim.
24. P. Maltsev, "Kto vinovat? . . . Nekotoryye voprosy organizatsii i osushchestvleniya upravleniya voyskami zapadnogo fronta nakamme i v nachal'nom periode voyny" [Who Is to Blame? . . . Certain Questions on the Organization and Implementation of Troop Command on the Western Front on the Eve and in the Initial Period of War], *Voyenno istoricheskly zhurnal,* no. 10 (1988), 21–28.
25. Ibid., 23.
26. Ibid., passim.
27. Ibid., 26.
28. Ibid.
29. Kunitsky, "Esli oborona prorvana . . . k vosstanovleniyu prorvannogo strategicheskogo fronta oborony na yugo–zapadnom napravlenii" [If Defense Is Disrupted: On Restoration of the Disrupted Strategic Defensive Front on the Southwestern Direction], *Voyenno istoricheskiy zhurnal,* no. 12 (1988), 3–10.
30. Ibid., 4.
31. Ibid. During the spring of 1942 Soviet forces had not yet developed the level of mastery with regard to strategic, operational, and tactical *maskirovka* that they would later acquire. See David M. Glantz, *Soviet Military Deception in the Second World War* (London: Frank Cass, 1989), 24.
32. Ibid., 2.
33. Ibid, 6.
34. Ibid.
35. The importance of this is stressed in Erickson, "Threat Assessment."
36. Richard K. Betts, *Surprise Attack: Lessons for Defense Planning* (Washington, DC: Brookings Institution, 1982). See also Ariel Levite, *Intelligence and Strategic Surprises* (New York: Columbia University Press, 1987); Betts, "Surprise, Scholasticism and Strategy: A Review of Ariel Levite's 'Intelligence and Strategic Surprises,' *International Studies Quarterly,* no. 33 (1989), 329–343, and Levite's response to Betts in the same issue, 345–349. See also Michael I. Handel, *Perception, Deception and Surprise* (Jerusalem: Leonard Davis Institute, Hebrew University of Jerusalem, 1976), and Handel, *War, Strategy and Intelligence* (London: Frank Cass, 1989), especially ch. 5, 229–281.
37. See John J. Mearsheimer, *Conventional Deterrence* (Ithaca, NY: Cornell University Press, 1983), ch. 2. Pertinent in Soviet military theory following the First World War is A. A. Svechin, *Strategiia* (Moscow: Voyenizdat,

1926), especially 250–268 in his discussion of the strategies of destruction and attrition [sokrusheniye and izmor]. I gratefully acknowledge Sally Stoecker for helpful insights here.

38. The case for limited nuclear options is argued by Albert Wohlstetter and Richard Brody, "Continuing Control as a Requirement for Deterring," ch. 5, in Ashton B. Carter, John D. Steinbruner, and Charles A. Zraket, eds., Managing Nuclear Operations (Washington, DC: Brookings Institution, 1987), 142–196. For counterarguments, see Robert Jervis, The Meaning of the Nuclear Revolution: Statecraft and the Prospect of Armageddon (Ithaca, NY: Cornell University Press, 1989), chs. 2–3.

39. Handel, War, Strategy and Intelligence, 238. For other cases and theory, see Klaus Knorr and Patrick M. Morgan, eds., Strategic Military Surprise (New Brunswick, NJ: Transaction Books, 1983).

40. Handel, Ibid.

41. Ibid., 239. See Richard Ned Lebow, Between Peace and War: The Nature of Brinkmanship Crises (Baltimore, MD: Johns Hopkins University Press, 1981) on the nature of brinkmanship crises. Lebow finds a significant number of historical cases in which a state's commitment was challenged by another on the assumption that the first state would yield, an assumption which flew in the face of a great deal of information to the contrary.

42. M. A. Gareev, M. V. Frunze—Voyennyy teoretik (M. V. Frunze: Military Theorist) (New York: Pergamon–Brassey's, 1988, English version), 208.

43. Andrey Kokoshin and Valentin Larionov, "Kurskaya bitva v svete sovremennoye oboronitel'noye doktriny" [The Battle of Kursk in View of Contemporary Defensive Doctrine], Miroyaya ekonomika i mezhdunarodnyye otnosheniya, no. 8 (1987), 32–40.

44. See P. H. Vigor, Soviet Blitzkrieg Theory (New York: St. Martin's Press, 1983); and M. M. Kir'yan, ed., Vnezapnost' v nastupatel'nykh operatsiyakh velikoy Otechestvennoy voyny [Surprise in Offensive Operations of the Great Patriotic War] (Moscow: 'Nauka,' 1986).

45. David M. Glantz, Colossus Reborn: The Red Army at War, 1941–1943 (Lawrence: University Press of Kansas, 2005), 614.

46. Ibid., 615. See also, on factors related to the transformation of the Red Army, Ibid., 136–137.

47. Glantz, Soviet Military Deception in the Second World War, 583. Glantz draws extensively on Kir'yan, Vnezapnost'. For a typology of deception, see Handel, War, Strategy and Intelligence, 315.

48. Glantz, Soviet Military Deception in the Second World War, 584.

49. Ibid.

50. Ibid., 584–585. See also Donnelly, Red Banner, ch. 8, 135–170.

51. Glantz, Soviet Military Deception in the Second World War, 586.

52. Types of deception are discussed in Handel, War, Strategy and Intelligence, ch. 7. See also May, ed., Knowing One's Enemies, 503–542, for the editor's summary of intelligence failures in estimating capabilities and "proclivities."

53. Richards J. Heuer, Jr., "Soviet Organization and Doctrine for Strategic Deception," ch. 2, in Brian D. Dailey and Patrick J. Parker, eds., Soviet Strategic Deception (Lexington, MA: Lexington Books, 1987), 21–54. See also, in the same volume, John J. Dziak, "Soviet Deception: The Organizational and Operational Tradition," ch. 1, 3–20; Richard H. Shultz and Roy Godson, Dezinformatsia: Active Measures in Soviet Strategy (New York: Pergamon–Brassey's, 1984). According to Ladislav Bittman,

Soviet intelligence agencies distinguish three types of "special operations," which U.S. analysts would call active measures: disinformation, propaganda, and influence operations. Bittman, *The Deception Game* (New York: Ballantine Books, 1972), 19 and passim.

54. Heuer, "Organization and Doctrine for Deception," 42.

55. Ibid., 43; Glantz, *Soviet Military Deception in the Second World War,* notes that Soviet experience in the Second World War demonstrated to Soviet planners the essential unity of all types of deception at the tactical, operational and strategic levels, ch. 7, 559ff. Strategic deception may be a special case on account of the high stakes and involvement of senior-level policy makers: see Handel, *War, Strategy and Intelligence,* ch. 8 on strategic and operational deception, especially his discussion of the strategic and operational deception plans by Allenby in Palestine in 1917 and the similarity of the latter to successful Second World War deceptions (366–367).

56. Handel, *War, Strategy and Intelligence,* 387, also notes: "During the shorter wars of the future, deceivers may not have the time to implement intricate deception operations; instead, cover plans will have to be prepared *before the outbreak of war in order to be used in its initial stages and may be much more difficult to apply at later stages.*"

57. My discussion of the Manchurian operation is derived from Glantz, *August Storm: The Soviet 1945 Strategic Offensive in Manchuria* (Ft. Leavenworth, KS: Combat Studies Institute, February 1983); Lilita 1. Dzirkals, *Lighting War in Manchuria: Soviet Military Analysis of the 1945 Far East Campaign* (Santa Monica, CA: RAND Corporation, 1976); Glantz, *August Storm: Soviet Tactical and Operational Combat in Manchuria, 1945* (Ft. Leavenworth, KS: Combat Studies Institute, June 1983); and Peter H. Vigor, *Soviet Blitzkrieg Theory* (New York: St. Martin's Press, 1983), ch. 9, 102–121. Important Soviet sources include Ivanov, ed., *Nachal'nyy period voyny* [The Initial Period of War], ch. 12; and Panov, Kiselev, Kartavtsev, et al., *Istoriya Voyennogo Iskusstva,* ch. 9.

58. Glantz, *August Storm: The Soviet 1945 Strategic Offensive in Manchuria,* ch. 1. According to S. P. Ivanov, chief of staff of the Soviet Far East Command in August 1945, the Transbaikal Front had four combined arms armies, a tank army, a group of Soviet–Mongolian troops, an air army, an air defense army, in addition to reinforcement formations and other support. Its total complement included 654,000 men, 7,000 guns and mortars, 2,416 tanks and self-propelled guns, 1,360 antitank guns, 601 antiaircraft guns, 583 rocket launchers, and 1,334 aircraft. Ivanov, *The Initial Period of War* (translated and published in U.S. Air Force, Soviet Military Thought Series, Washington, DC: U.S. Government Printing Office, 1986), 250. The Far East Command structure and order of battle are given by Glantz, *August Storm,* Appendix 2, 199–213. In addition to the forces of three *fronts,* the Soviets also employed maritime forces from the Amur Flotilla and the Pacific Fleet. Operational statistics, including the width of attack frontage, depth of advance and tempo of advance for the three main fronts of the Soviet attack in Manchuria are enumerated in Glantz, *August Storm,* Appendix 3, 215–216, and 44–47. Chief of staff of the Transbaikal Front Gen. M. V. Zakharov has written extensively about the Manchurian campaign, see Zakharov, ed., *Final: istoriko memuarny ocherk o razgrome irnperialisticheskoy iapony v*

1945 godu [Finale: A Historical Memoir Record of the Rout of Imperialist Japan in 1945] (Moscow: 'Nauka,' 1969).

59. Glantz, *August Storm,* 39, and Dzirkals, *Lightning War,* 38–39, and Appendix A. Dzirkals notes that the position of Far East commander in chief was not officially created until July 30, 1945, "after Vasilevskiy's first weeks on location had proven that his authority as STAVKA representative was insufficient." (Ibid., 39). As we have seen, in the earliest stages of the war against Germany (June–July 1941) Soviet forces in the West were organized into three large *fronts,* which were de facto theater commands. These commands were subsequently broken into smaller commands, which became directly subordinated to the STAVKA, Supreme High Command, and the Soviets did not return to the early system until the closing stages of the war. See Ibid., 38; and General of the Army S. Shtemenko, "Triumph of Soviet Military Strategy," *New Times,* no. 18 (May 1975), 5, cited by Dzirkals.

60. Ivanov, *Initial Period of War,* 253.

61. Glantz, *August Storm,* 4.

62. Ivanov, *Initial Period of War,* 261.

63. Ibid.

64. Handel, *War, Strategy and Intelligence,* ch. 5, page 234 notes that modern technology has offsetting effects on the surpriser and intended victim. Familiarity with blitzkrieg tactics and photographic and electronic reconnaissance aid defenders reduce the probability of surprise, especially surprise "out of the blue." Conversely, nuclear weapons and high-technology conventional weapons make it theoretically possible for one side to win a decisive victory within minutes. The balance is not entirely equal, however: despite technology favoring the defense, the basic problems of surprise are not technological but psychological and perceptual. See also his chapter on "Technological Surprise in War," 131–183 in the same volume, and his comments in the introduction to Handel, ed., *Clausewitz and Modern Strategy* (London: Frank Cass, 1986).

65. Cited in Stephen J. Blank, *Threats to Russian Security: The View from Moscow* (Carlisle Barracks, PA: U.S. Army War College, Strategic Studies Institute, July 2000), 10.

66. Richard H. Phillips, "Problems in Soviet Tactical Training," *Soviet Defense Notes,* no. 4 (July 1990), 5–8, indicates a carryover from Soviet practices in the Second World War to a roteness in the conduct of exercises even today. Critiques of Soviet exercises for their lack of imagination and rigid adherence to formula have marked the Soviet military press for many years.

67. I am grateful to Timothy Thomas for this point. He is not responsible for its application here.

68. Paul Bracken emphasizes this point with regard to military organizations. See Bracken, "Institutional Factors in War Termination," ch. 7, in Stephen J. Cimbala and Sidney R. Waldman, eds., *Controlling and Ending Conflict: Issues Before and After the Cold War* (Westport, CT: Greenwood Press, 1991), 183–196.

69. Vladimir Yakovlev, commander in chief, Russian Strategic Nuclear Forces, December 1999, cited in Blank, *Threats to Russian Security,* 11–12.

70. Nekrich, *1941 Iyunya,* 217–223.

71. See "Afghanistan: First Lessons," in *Jane's Defense Weekly,* December 19, 2001, and "Afghanistan: The Key Lessons," *Jane's Defence Weekly,*

January 2, 2002, for an assessment of U.S. military operations in Afghanistan. I am grateful to Robert David Steele for calling this to my attention. For additional background, see Chris Bellamy, *The Future of Land Warfare* (New York: St. Martin's Press, 1987), chs. 6–7. For a discussion by expert Soviet analysts, see D. A. Ivanov, V. P. Savel'yev, and P. V. Shemanski, *Osnovy upravleniya voyskami v boyu* [Fundamentals of Troop Control in Battle] (Moscow: Voyenizdat, 1977), 52–53.

Chapter 2: Russia and Military Transformation: Perspectives from the First Nuclear Age

1. Informative essays on this topic appear in MacGregor Knox and Williamson Murray, eds., *The Dynamics of Military Revolution 1300–2050* (Cambridge: Cambridge University Press, 2001), especially 1–14 and 175–194.
2. Raymond L. Garthoff, *The Great Transition: American-Soviet Relations and the End of the Cold War* (Washington, DC: Brookings Institution, 1994), especially 551–598.
3. Garthoff, *Deterrence and the Revolution in Soviet Military Doctrine* (Washington, DC: Brookings Institution, 1990), 6–28, is especially helpful on these points. Other sources pertinent to Soviet deterrence concepts are cited in notes that follow.
4. David Holloway, *Stalin and the Bomb: The Soviet Union and Atomic Energy, 1939–1956* (New Haven, CT: Yale University Press, 1994), 253. Although Stalin emphasized the development of delivery vehicles for Soviet atomic weapons and defense against atomic attack, he did not regard the atomic bomb as a decisive weapon. Ibid., 250.
5. Harriet Fast Scott and William F. Scott, *Soviet Military Doctrine: Continuity, Formulation, and Dissemination* (Boulder, CO: Westview Press, 1988), passim.
6. Speech of Comrade G. M. Malenkov, *Pravda*, March 13, 1954, cited in Yuri Smirnov and Vladislav Zubok, "Nuclear Weapons after Stalin's Death: Moscow Enters the H-Bomb Age," *Cold War International History Project*, retrieved from http://cwihp.si.edu/cwihplib.nsf/, November 6, 2000.
7. Smirnov and Zubok, "Nuclear Weapons after Stalin's Death," op. cit.
8. Ibid.
9. V. D. Sokolovskiy, ed., *Voennaya Strategiya* [Military Strategy] (Moscow: Voenizdat, 1962) illustrates the impact of Khrushchev's views of the priority of nuclear-missile war on officially approved military doctrine. Later editions of this work were published in 1963 and 1968. See also Scott and Scott, *Soviet Military Doctrine*, 34–41.
10. Evolution of the Soviet definition of victory in the Cold War years is traced in A. A. Kokoshin, V. M. Sergeev, and V. L. Tsymbursky, "Evolution of the Concept of 'Victory' in Soviet Military: Political Thought after World War II," Paper presented at workshop sponsored by the Committee on Contributions of Behavioral and Social Science to the Prevention of Nuclear War, Commission on Behavioral and Social Sciences and Education, National Research Council (Talinn, Estonia: January 1999).
11. The 1964 Warsaw Pact plan was brought to light by the Parallel History Project under the direction of Vojtech Mastny. For his commentary on the plan, see the PHP, http://www.isn.ethz.ch/php/documents/introvm.htm.
12. Vojtech Mastny, "Taking Lyon on the Ninth Day? The 1964 Warsaw Pact Plan for a Nulcear War in Europe and Related Documents," Introduction, 2, http://www.isn.ethz.ch/php/documents/introvm.htm.

13. Pyotr Ivashutin, "Strategic Operations of the Nuclear Forces," August 28, 1964, 9, http://www.isn.ethz.ch/php/documents/1/ivashutin-engl.htm.
14. Jennifer G. Mathers, *The Russian Nuclear Shield from Stalin to Yeltsin* (London: Macmillan, 2000), 25–28.
15. Andrei A. Kokoshin, *Soviet Strategic Thought, 1917–91* (Cambridge, MA: MIT Press, 1998), 124. See also Zisk, *Engaging the Enemy*, 47–81 on Soviet reactions to NATO flexible response strategy.
16. Kokoshin, *Soviet Strategic Thought*, 126.
17. Ibid., 127.
18. Ghulam Dastagir Wardak, comp., and Graham Hall Turbiville, Jr., ed., *The Voroshilov Lectures: Materials from the Soviet General Staff Academy, Vol. I* (Washington, DC: National Defense University Press, 1989), 233–254.
19. Ibid., 244–245.
20. Ibid, 245.
21. Ibid., 245–246.
22. Ibid., 247. This is one clue to apparent Soviet unwillingness to accept U.S. versions of controlled nuclear escalation, as for example in National Security Decision Memorandum (NSDM) 242, later referred to as the "Schlesinger Doctrine."
23. Ben B. Fischer, *A Cold War Conundrum: The 1983 Soviet War Scare* (Washington, DC: U.S. Central Intelligence Agency, Center for the Study of Intelligence, September 1997), 24–26, provides an informative account of Able Archer and its presumed relationship to Soviet fears of war.
24. Gordon Brook-Shepherd, *The Storm Birds: Soviet Postwar Defectors* (New York: Wiedenfeld and Nicolson, 1989), 329.
25. Ibid., 330–331.
26. See Graham H. Turbiville, Jr., "Strategic Deployment: Mobilizing and Moving the Force," *Military Review*, no. 68 (December 1988), 41–49. According to the first volume of the Voroshilov Military Academy of the General Staff lecture materials of the 1970s, "the notification by alert given to bring the strategic nuclear forces to full combat readiness, is only some minutes, while for the units, large units, and operational formations of the various Services of the Armed Forces, such notification will be longer to a greater extent." *Voroshilov Lectures, I,* 181. On the levels of combat readiness (*boevoy gotovnost'*) and the process of bringing the Soviet armed forces to full combat readiness, see Ibid., ch. 4. Although the process of bringing the armed forces to the highest level of combat readiness "should be conducted under all conditions in close consideration of the employment of nuclear weapons by the enemy" and "control should ensure centralized and simultaneous communication of signals and instructions" according to measures developed by the General Staff and made known to the troops. (Ibid., 193–194).
27. Stephen Shenfield, "Crisis Management: the Soviet Approach," ch. 18, in Carl Jacobsen, ed., *Strategic Power: USA/USSR* (New York: Macmillan, 1990), 198–205, citation 200. See also the discussion in the next chapter on Soviet versus American views of crisis management.
28. Bruce G. Blair, *The Logic of Accidental Nuclear War* (Washington, DC: Brookings Institution, 1993), especially 25–26.
29. Stephen M. Meyer, "Soviet Nuclear Operations," ch. 15, in Ashton B. Carter, John D. Steinbruner, and Charles A. Zraket, eds., *Managing Nuclear Operations* (Washington, DC: Brookings Institution, 1987), 470–534.

30. Ibid., 513–516.
31. *Voroshilov Lectures, I,* 181.
32. Ibid., 229. Soviet military writers also use the term "strategic leadership" [*stratigicheskaya rukovodstva*] to refer to the highest political and military leaders as a group. Prior to 1987 this was assumed to be the Defense Council, a smaller body within the Politburo, and it was supposed that in wartime the Defense Council assumed the same functions and authority as had the GKO (State Committee for Defense) in World War II. Under Gorbachev realignments of power among party, government, and armed forces after 1987, there was more guesswork involved in extrapolating from Soviet peacetime to wartime command arrangements. For pertinent background, see Harriet Fast and William F. Scott, *The Soviet Control Structure: Capabilities for Wartime Survival* (New York: Crane, Russak/National Strategy Information Center, 1983), 45–58.
33. *Voroshilov Lectures, I,* 229.
34. Ibid., 231.
35. Soviet General Staff discussion and debate over the issue of limited strategic nuclear war is considered in Kimberley Marten Zisk, *Engaging the Enemy: Organization Theory and Soviet Military Innovation, 1955–1991* (Princeton, NJ: Princeton University Press, 1993), 98–119. For additional discussion of limited nuclear war, see Edward L. Warner III, *Soviet Concepts and Capabilities for Limited Nuclear War: What We Know and How We Know It* (Santa Monica, CA: RAND Corporation, February 1989). This study contains many important primary source references. See also A. I. Yevseev, "O nekotorykh tendentsiyakh v izmenenii soderzhaniya i kharaktera nachal'nogo perioda voiny," *Voenno-istoricheskii zhurnal,* no. 11 (November 1985), 10–20. Writing of the impact of a massive nuclear strike at the outset of a war, Yevseev notes that "the initial period of a future nuclear-rocket war may be the fundamental and decisive period which in large measure predetermines the further development of armed conflict, and in certain conditions the outcome of war." (Yevseyev, "O nekorotykh tendentsiyakh," 17).
36. Desmond Ball, *Soviet Strategic Planning and the Control of Nuclear War* (Canberra: Strategic and Defence Studies Centre, Australian National University, November 1983), 5. See also page 8 for his notional RISOP table.
37. Ibid., 5.
38. Garthoff, *Deterrence and the Revolution in Soviet Military Doctrine,* especially 52 and passim; and David Holloway, *The Soviet Union and the Arms Race,* 2nd Edition (New Haven, CT: Yale University Press, 1983), especially 43–52.
39. See the opening Soviet statement at the SALT I negotiations, as quoted in Holloway, *The Soviet Union and the Arms Race,* 46.
40. For example, Marshal of the Soviet Union N. V. Ogarkov, *Istoriya uchit bditel'nosti* (Moscow: Voenizdat, 1985), 75–77. See especially page 77 for Ogarkov's emphasis on Soviet "no first use" policy with regard to nuclear weapons and his pejorative reference to U.S. nomenclature of strategic "offensive" forces. See also his discussion of U.S. plans for limited nuclear war in Europe and for building up U.S. strategic forces under Reagan. Ibid., 68.
41. Mathers, *The Russian Nuclear Shield from Stalin to Yeltsin,* 74–75.

42. See, for example: Andrei Kokoshin, "Nuclear Arms Reduction and Strategic Stability," SShA: *Ekonomika, politika, ideologiya*, no. 2 (February
1988), 3–12, FBIS-SOV-88-051, March 16, 1988; Alexei Arbatov, "Parity and Reasonable Sufficiency," *International Affairs* (English version),
no. 10 (October 1988), 75–87; Arbatov, "How Much Defence Is Sufficient?" *International Affairs* (English version), no. 4 (1989), 31–44;
Lev Semeiko, "Razumnaya dostatochnost'—put' k nadezhnomy miry"
[Reasonable Sufficiency—Path to Reliable Peace], *Kommunist*, no. 7
(May 1989), 112–121.

43. Vitaliy Zhurkin, Sergei Karaganov, and Andrei Kortunov, "Security Challenges: Old and New," *Kommunist*, no. 1 (January 1988), 42–50, JPRS-
UKO-88-006, March 24, 1988.

44. Daniil Proektor, "Politics, Clausewitz and Victory in Nuclear War," *International Affairs* (English version), no. 5 (1988), 74–80. A large debate
about politics and nuclear war had been stimulated by an earlier article
in the same journal: see Boris Kanevsky and Pyotr Shabardin, "The Correlation of Politics, War and a Nuclear Catastrophe," *International Affairs* (English version), no. 2 (1988), 95–104.

45. Graham Allison, Ashton B. Carter, Steven E. Miller, and Philip Zelikow,
Cooperative Denuclearization: From Pledges to Deeds (Cambridge, MA:
Center for Science and International Affairs, Harvard University, January
1993). See also William C. Martel and William T. Pendley, *Nuclear Coexistence: Rethinking U.S. Policy to Promote Stability in an Era of Proliferation* (Montgomery, AL: Air War College, April 1994), especially 49–66.

46. See, in particular, Glantz, ed., *The Initial Period of War*.

47. Suvorov, quoted in V.Ye. Savkin, *Osnovnye printsipy operativnogo
iskusstva i taktiki* (Moscow: Voenizdat, 1972), translated in U.S. Air
Force Soviet Military Thought Series as *The Basic Principles of Operational Art and Tactics* (Washington, DC: U.S. Government Printing Office, undated), 244.

48. See, in particular, Scott and Scott, *Soviet Military Doctrine*, 110–115.

49. Marshal N.V. Ogarkov, *Vsegda v gotovnosti k zashchite Otechestva* (Moscow: Voenizdat, 1982), 34.

50. Ibid., 16.

51. Ogarkov, *Istoriya uchit bditel'nosti*, 68–69.

52. V.G. Reznichenko, et al., *Taktika* [Tactics] (Moscow: Voenizdat, 1984),
translated by CIS Multilingual Section, National Defense Headquarters,
Ottawa, Canada, 69.

53. Ibid., 67.

54. Ibid.

55. Ibid.

56. On partial surprise, see Vigor, *Soviet Blitzkrieg Theory*, 156–157 and
passim.

57. M.A. Gareev, *M.V. Frunze: Voennyi teoretik* [M.V. Frunze: Military Theo-
rist] (New York: Pergamon–Brassey's, 1988, English version), 208.

58. Andrey Kokoshin and Valentin Larionov, "Kurskaya bitva v svete
sovremennoye oboronitel'noye doctriny," *Mirovaya ekonomika i
mezhdunarodnyye otnosheniya*, no. 8 (1987), 32–40.

59. Gareev, *M.V. Frunze*, 216. Gareev cites V. D. Sokolovskiy, ed., *Voennaya
strategiya* (Moscow: Voenizdat, 1963), 22.

60. Michael MccGwire, *Military Objectives in Soviet Foreign Policy* (Washington, DC: Brookings Institution, 1987), chs. 2–3.

61. See John G. Hines and Phillip A. Petersen, "The Changing Soviet System of Control for Theater War," *International Defense Review*, no. 3 (March 1986), revised in Stephen J. Cimbala, ed., *Soviet C3* (Washington, DC: AFCEA International Press, 1987), 191–219; Hines, Petersen, and Notra Trulock III, "Soviet Military Theory from 1945–2000: Implications for NATO," *The Washington Quarterly*, no. 4 (1986), 117–137; and Raymond L. Garthoff, "Mutual Deterrence, Parity and Strategic Arms Limitation in Soviet Policy," ch. 5, in Derek Leebaert, ed., *Soviet Military Thinking* (London: Allen and Unwin, 1981), 92–124.

62. Gareev, *M.V. Frunze*, 216.

63. Ibid.

64. See Marshal of the Soviet Union and former Defense Minster Sergei Akhromeyev, "Doktrina predotvrashcheniya voiny, zashchity mira i sotsializma"[Doctrine for the Prevention of War, the Defense of Peace and Socialism] *Problemy mira i sotsializma*, 12 (December 1987), 23–28.

65. Kipp, "Soviet War Planning," in Glantz, ed., *The Initial Period of War on the Eastern Front*, 40–50, citation 49.

66. *Voroshilov Lectures, I*, 205–232.

67. V. G. Reznichenko, et al., *Taktika* [Tactics] (Moscow: Voenizdat, 1987), 20.

68. Ibid., 21.

69. D. T. Yazov, "Novaya model' bezopasnosti i vooruzhennyye sily" [A New Model of Security and the Armed Forces] *Kommunist*, 18 (December 1989), 61–72.

70. Ibid., 66.

71. Dale R. Herspring, *The Soviet High Command, 1967–1989: Personalities and Politics* (Princeton, NJ: Princeton University Press, 1990), 265–276. See also Garthoff, *The Great Transition,* 528–530.

72. Nicolai N. Petro and Alvin Z. Rubinstein, *Russian Foreign Policy: From Empire to Nation-State* (New York: Longman, 1997), 151.

73. George M. Mellinger, "Survey: The Military Year 1989 in Review," in Mellinger, ed., *Soviet Armed Forces Review Annual*, 1989, vol. 13 (Gulf Breeze, FL: Academic International Press, 1995), 2.

74. Thomas M. Nichols, *The Sacred Cause: Civil-Military Conflict over Soviet National Security 1917–1992* (Ithaca, NY: Cornell University Press, 1993). On the failed coup of August, 1991, see John B. Dunlop, *The Rise of Russia and the Fall of the Soviet Empire* (Princeton, NJ: Princeton University Press, 1993), 186–255, especially 247–250.

75. The Conflict Studies Research Centre, Royal Military Academy Sandhurst, provides updated military assessments of events in Chechnya. See, for example, C.W. Blandy, *Chechnya: Two Federal Disasters* (Camberley: CSRC, Royal Military Academy Sandhurst, April 2002).

Chapter 3: Russian Nuclear Command and Control and Stable Deterrence

1. See, for example, Peter Vincent Pry, *War Scare: Russia and America on the Nuclear Brink* (Westport, CT: Praeger Publishers, 1999). For purposes of this discussion and in the interest of brevity, we use the term C3 system to include C3I systems (command, control, communications, and intelligence) or C4I systems (command, control, communications, computers, and intelligence).

2. Bruce G. Blair, "We Keep Building Nukes for All the Wrong Reasons," *Washington Post*, May 25, 2003; Johnson's Russia List no. 7198, May 28, 2003, davidjohnson@erols.com; Statement by former Senator Sam Nunn,

cochairman, Nuclear Threat Initiative, www.nti.org, on RAND report *Beyond the Nuclear Shadow*, May 21, 2003, CDI Russia Weekly no. 258, May 23, 2003, Center for Defense Information, djohnson@cdi.org; full text of RAND report is at www.rand.org/publications/MR/MR1666/; Bruce Blair, "The Impact of National Missile Defense on Russia and Nuclear Security," *The Defense Monitor*, no. 8 (December 1, 2000), http://www.cdi.org/dm/2000/issue8/nmdrussia.html.

3. Peter Douglas Feaver, *Guarding the Guardians: Civilian Control of Nuclear Weapons in the United States* (Ithaca, NY: Cornell University Press, 1992), 12.

4. John D. Steinbruner, "Choices and Trade-offs," ch. 16, in Carter, Steinbruner, and Zraket, eds., *Managing Nuclear Operations* (Washington, DC: Brookings Institution, 1987), 535–554, especially 539–541.

5. On the relationship between deterrence and stress, see Richard Ned Lebow and Janice Gross Stein, *We All Lost the Cold War* (Princeton, NJ: Princeton University Press, 1994) 331–338.

6. Scott D. Sagan, *Moving Targets: Nuclear Strategy and National Security* (Princeton, NJ: Princeton University Press, 1989), 164–165.

7. Ibid.

8. Bruce G. Blair, *The Logic of Accidental Nuclear War* (Washington, DC: Brookings Institution, 1993), passim.; Blair, *Strategic Command and Control: Redefining the Nuclear Threat* (Washington, DC: Brookings Institution, 1985), 65–78. Blair's 1993 book is the most detailed on operations of the Soviet and now Russian nuclear C3 systems.

9. Steinbruner, "Choices and Trade-offs," in Carter, Steinbruner and Zraket, eds., *Managing Nuclear Operations*, 542–543.

10. Graham T. Allison, *Essence of Decision* (Boston: Little, Brown, 1971), 137.

11. Ashton B. Carter, "Sources of Error and Uncertainty," ch. 18, in Carter, Steinbruner, and Zraket, eds., *Managing Nuclear Operations*, 628.

12. Charles Perrow, *Normal Accidents: Living with High-Risk Technologies* (New York: Basic Books, 1984). Perrow's concept is further developed and applied to nuclear accident theory in Scott D. Sagan, *The Limits of Safety: Organizations, Accidents and Nuclear Weapons* (Princeton, NJ: Princeton University Press, 1993), 31–36.

13. Sagan, *The Limits of Safety*, 34; Perrow, *Normal Accidents*, 93–96.

14. But see Sagan, *The Limits of Safety*, 228–246.

15. Ibid., 248.

16. Feaver, *Guarding the Guardians*, 38.

17. I suspect that Russian nuclear force commanders are worried about Ivan and Boris in this regard; if not, they ought to be, given the current morale of the Russian military. Russian defense minister Igor Rodionov declared in January 1997 that the possibility of a breakdown in the nuclear command and control system was very real.

18. Paul Bracken, *The Command and Control of Nuclear Forces* (New Haven, CT: Yale University Press, 1983), 196.

19. Blair, *The Logic of Accidental Nuclear War*, 91.

20. Ibid., 85.

21. Blair, interview "Russian Roulette," *Frontline*, 8–9.

22. Blair, "The Impact of National Missile Defense on Russia and Nuclear Security," 1.

23. Ibid., 3.

Chapter 4: Missile Defenses and U.S.-Russian Relations

1. Nikolai Sokov, "The ABM Treaty: The End of One Saga and the Start of Another," *PONARS Policy Memo No. 218* (Washington, DC: Center for Strategic and International Studies, January 25, 2002), 47–51.

2. "U.S., Russia Agree to Reduce Nuclear Arms," CNN.com/U.S., May 14, 2002, http://europe.cnn.com/2002/U.S./05/13/bush.nuclear/index.html.

3. "NATO to Seal New Pact with Russia," CNN.com /WORLD, May 14, 2002, http://europe.cnn.com/2002/WORLD/europe/05/14/iceland.nato/index.html.

4. Pavel Podvig, ed., *Russian Strategic Nuclear Forces* (Cambridge, MA: MIT Press, 2001), 28.

5. Ibid.

6. Ibid., 30.

7. Ibid.

8. Matthew G. McKinzie, Thomas B. Cochran, Robert S. Norris, and William M. Arkin, *The U.S. Nuclear War Plan: A Time for Change* (Washington, DC: Natural Resources Defense Council, June 2001), 11.

9. Ibid., 12.

10. For an argument that the SIOP is passé and what to do about it, see the briefing by Robert S. Norris, *Abolishing the U.S. Nuclear War Plan*, Presentation to the Carnegie International Non-Proliferation Conference (Washington, DC: June 18–19, 2001). See also Robert S. McNamara, "Reflections on War in the Twenty-First Century: The Context for Nuclear Abolition," ch. 10, in John Baylis and Robert O'Neill, eds., *Alternative Nuclear Futures: The Role of Nuclear Weapons in the Post-Cold War World* (Oxford: Oxford University Press, 2000), 167–182.

11. Natural Resources Defense Council, *Nuclear Weapons and Waste: In Depth Report: the U.S. Nuclear War Plan: A Time For Change* (Washington, DC: Natural Resources Defense Council, 2001), Executive Summary, 1, http://www.nrdc.org/nuclear/warplan/execsum.asp.

12. Ibid., 2.

13. This was the so-called window of vulnerability argument asserted in the 1970s and 1980s by the Committee on the Present Danger and by some Carter and Reagan officials. The argument assumed that the side lacking counterforce equivalence with its competitor would be vulnerable to intimidation in a crisis on account of the expectation that, if deterrence failed, the nuclear war fighting potential of the stronger side (in deployable counterforce or prompt counterforce) would allow the stronger side to prevail.

    However, this assumption of prevailing in nuclear war (1) assumed survivable and enduring command and control that were far beyond the competency of U.S. or Soviet technology, (2) neglected the co-location of military and civilian targets, and (3) usually omitted any requirement for active defenses (without which a "countervailing" strategy for prevailing based on counterforce supremacy led to a dead end, unless one side surrendered almost immediately). For nonpolemical discussions of the history of U.S. and Soviet or Russian missile defenses, see Donald R. Baucom, *The Origins of SDI, 1944–1983* (Lawrence: University Press of Kansas, 1992); and Jennifer G. Mathers, *The Russian Nuclear Shield from Stalin to Yeltsin* (London: Macmillan, 2000).

14. Secretary of Defense Donald Rumsfeld, *Memorandum on Missile Defense Program Direction* (Washington, DC: Office of the Secretary of Defense,

January 2, 2002). See also "DOD Establishes Missile Defense Agency," News Release, Department of Defense, January 4, 2002, DODNEWS-L@DTIC.MIL.

15. For a similar argument on behalf of limited U.S. NMD, see Michael E. O'Hanlon, *Defense Policy Choices for the Bush Administration 2000–5* (Washington, DC: Brookings Institution Press, 2001), 143–176.

Chapter 5: Russia and Nuclear Proliferation: Fateful Choices and Rational Decision

1. Kenneth N. Waltz, *Theory of International Politics* (Reading, MA: Addison-Wesley, 1979). See also, and more specifically on Waltz's views of the relationship between nuclear weapons and stability: *The Spread of Nuclear Weapons: More May Be Better,* Adelphi Papers no. 171 (London: International Institute of Strategic Studies, 1981); "Nuclear Myths and Political Realities," *American Political Science Review,* no. 3 (September 1990), 731–745; and his chapters in Scott D. Sagan and Kenneth N. Waltz, *The Spread of Nuclear Weapons: A Debate* (New York: Norton, 1995). Other arguments for a positive association between the spread of survivable nuclear forces and international stability appear in Martin Van Creveld, *Nuclear Proliferation and the Future of Conflict* (New York: Free Press, 1993).

2. For a sorting of realist views on international politics, see John J. Mearsheimer, *The Tragedy of Great Power Politics* (New York: Norton, 2001), especially 14–22. See also Hans J. Morgenthau, *Politics among Nations: The Struggle for Power and Peace* (New York: Knopf, 1948). Paul R. Viotti and Mark V. Kauppi divide international political theories into realist, pluralist, and globalist schools, a taxonomy similar to that offered by Kalevi J. Holsti. See Viotti and Kauppi, eds., *International Relations Theory: Realism, Pluralism, Globalism* (New York: Macmillan, 1993), especially ch. 1, 61–227; and Holsti, *Peace and War: Armed Conflicts and International Order* (Cambridge: Cambridge University Press, 1991), 328. See also Holsti's comments on the roots of realism and neorealism, 329–330. An excellent summary and critique of neorealist views is provided by Robert O. Keohane, "Theory of World Politics: Structural Realism and Beyond," in Ada W. Finifter, ed., *Political Science: The State of the Discipline* (Washington, DC: American Political Science Association, 1983), and reprinted in Viotti and Kauppi, eds., *International Relations Theory,* 186–227.

3. Conversely, John Mearsheimer is correct to note that realism is inconsistent with much American public opinion and with a great deal of U.S. public diplomacy because it is "at odds with the deep-seated sense of optimism and moralism that pervades much of American society. Liberalism, on the other hand, fits neatly with those values." Mearsheimer, *The Tragedy of Great Power Politics,* 23. Realism/neorealism is contrasted with liberalism/neoliberal institutionalism and radical/dependency perspectives as competing perspectives on state policy in Karen Mingst, *Essentials of International Relations* (New York: Norton, 2003), 129, and passim.

4. The term "system" has many uses in international politics and in political science. Structural-realist theories of international politics emphasize the causal importance of system *structure*: numbers and types of units in the system and the distribution of military and other capabilities among those units. Other variations of systems theory emphasize the

interactions among components of the system, including the *interdependence* of the actors or units. For a concise discussion of systemic theories of international politics, see James E. Dougherty and Robert L. Pfaltzgraff, Jr., *Contending Theories of International Politics, Fourth Edition* (New York: Longman, 1997), 100–134.

5. Mearsheimer's capstone defense of offensive realism, *The Tragedy of Great Power Politics,* passim, provides ample evidence for this point. Vital interests as used here refers to interests over which states resist compromise and for which they are willing to go to war. See Donald M. Snow, *National Security: Defense Policy in a Changed International Order* (New York: St. Martin's Press, 1998), 173–180.

6. Robert Jervis, *System Effects: Complexity in Political and Social Life* (Princeton, NJ: Princeton University Press, 1998), 92–93, and passim.

7. Waltz, *Theory of International Politics,* 80.

8. Jervis, *System Effects,* 109.

9. See Morton Kaplan, *System and Process in International Politics* (New York: Wiley, 1957), for an early and pioneering effort for its time. International systems theories are classified and critiqued in Jervis, *System Effects,* ch. 3.

10. Waltz, "The Stability of a Bipolar World," *Deadalus,* 93 (Summer 1964), 881–909; and Waltz, *Theory of International Politics,* 170–171, cited in Jervis, *System Effects,* 118.

11. Mearsheimer, *The Tragedy of Great Power Politics,* 337 and passim.

12. David E. Sanger, "North Korea Says It Has a Program on Nuclear Arms," *New York Times,* October 17, 2002, A1, A12. See also James Dao, "The Pact That the Koreans Flouted," *New York Times,* October 17, 2002, A12.

13. Thomas A. Keaney and Eliot A. Cohen, *Revolution in Warfare? Air Power in the Persian Gulf* (Annapolis, MD: Naval Institute Press, 1995), 67. This is a revised version of the official U.S. Air Force *Gulf War Air Power Survey* (GWAPS) first published in 1993.

14. Keaney and Cohen, *Revolution in Warfare,* 67.

15. Ibid.

16. Ibid., 72.

17. Ibid., 75.

18. Ibid., 78. Special forces teams may have destroyed some mobile SCUDs.

19. Jeffrey Record, *Hollow Victory: A Contrary View of the Gulf War* (Washington, DC: Brassey's, 1993), 71–73.

20. Secretary of Defense William J. Perry, *On Ballistic Missile Defense: Excerpt from a Speech to the Chicago Council on Foreign Relations,* March 8, 1995, 1 (mimeo), cited in Keith B. Payne, *Deterrence in the Second Nuclear Age* (Lexington: University Press of Kentucky, 1996), 58.

21. Payne, *Deterrence in the Second Nuclear Age,* 57–58.

22. Rumsfeld Commission, *Report* (Executive Summary, 1998), 10.

23. Ibid, 11.

24. Ibid.

25. Ibid., 22. The Rumsfeld Commission cannot be dismissed by skeptics as an alarmist group. Its membership included, in addition to former Secretary of Defense Donald Rumsfeld who chaired it, noted experts on nuclear technology, strategy, and policy representing a variety of policy views and professional backgrounds.

26. Statement of the Honorable Douglas J. Feith, undersecretary of defense

for policy, to Senate Armed Services Committee, Hearing on Nuclear Posture Review, February 14, 2002, 3.

27. Michael R. Gordon, "Nuclear Arms: For Deterrence or Fighting?" *New York Times*, March 11, 2002, A1, A8.

28. The Russian legislator and Chinese academic are cited in Eric Schmitt, "U.S. Tries to Explain New Policy for A-Bomb," *New York Times*, March 11, 2002, A8.

29. One of the more controversial locutions to issue from the George W. Bush administration, the "Axis of Evil" was an attempt to warn of states that combined potential WMD threats with support of international terrorism. North Korea fits the WMD category of fears but its profile in terrorism is low, outside of South Korea.

30. In addition to Sagan's works cited earlier, see Sagan, "The Perils of Proliferation in South Asia," ch. 9, in Michael R. Chambers, ed., *South Asia in 2020: Future Strategic Balances and Alliances* (Carlisle Barracks, PA: U.S. Army War College, Strategic Studies Institute, November 2002), 191–227.

31. John G. Stoessinger, *Why Nations Go to War*, 8th Edition (New York: Bedford/St. Martin's Press, 2001), 1–23.

32. For abundant evidence, see Donald Kagan, *On the Origins of War and the Preservation of Peace* (New York: Anchor Books, 1996), 81–231.

Chapter 6: Russia's War in Chechnya, 1994-1996

1. Alan Stephens, "The Transformation of 'Low Intensity Conflict,'" *Small Wars and Insurgencies*, 5, no. 1 (Spring 1994), 143–161.

2. "S chego nachinalas' tragediia," *Orientir*, no. 3, (1995), 29–34.

3. Galina Koval'skaia, "Nepopravimoe. Kak i pochemu nachalas' chechenskaia voina," *Itogi*, June 18, 1996, 24–26.

4. N. N. Beliakov, "Voina v Chechne -puskovoi mekhanizm respada Rossii," in N. N. Beliakov, comp., *Chechenskii krizis* (March 1995), 37–41.

5. Chernov, "Krizis na Kavkaze mozhet privesti k obrazovaniiu novogo gorskogo gosudarstva," *Trud*, January 24, 1995.

6. Iuri Tyssovskii, "Kaspii: shchupal'tsia chuzhikh interesov," *Rossiia*, August 9–15, 1995.

7. "Chechenskii uzel. Na poroge voiny," *Izvestiia*, December 3, 1994.

8. Igor Korotchenko, "Operatsiia v Chechne. Uspekh ili porazhenie rossiiskoi armii," *Nezavisimoe voennoe obozrenie*, no. 1 (February 1995), 1.

9. Raymond C. Finch III, "Why the Russian Military Failed in Chechnya," e-version retrieved from www.amina.com/article.

10. Timothy L. Thomas, "Air Operation in Low Intensity Conflict: The Case of Chechnya," e-version retrieved from www.amina.com/article/thomas_mili.html.

11. Pavel Baev, *The Russian Army in a Time of Troubles* (Thousand Oaks, CA: Sage, 1996), 143.

12. Sergei Surozhtsev, "Legendarnaiia v Groznom," *Novoe vremia*, nos. 2–3 (1995), 14–15.

13. N. N. Novichkov, V. Ya. Snegovskii, and A. G. Sokolov, *Rossiiskie vooruzhennye sily v chechnskom konflikte. Analiz, itogi, vyvody* (Paris, Moscow, 1995), 118.

14. Andrew Wilson, "Russian Military Haunted by Past Glories. Battle to Improve Slumming Morale and Poor Performance," *Jane's International*

Defense Review, no. 5 (1996), 25–27.
15. Novichkov, Snegovskii, and Sokolov, *Rossiiskie vooruzhennye sily v chechnskom konflikte. Analiz, itogi, vyvody*, 117.
16. Richard Woff, "Who's Who in the Chechen Operation," *Jane's Intelligence Review*, 7, no. 4 (1995), 158–161.
17. Anatol Lieven, *Chechnya: Tombstone of Russian Power* (New Haven, CT: Yale University Press, 1998), 106.
18. Pavel K. Baev, "The Russian Army and Chechnya: Victory Instead of Reform?" ch. 4, in Stephen J. Cimbala, ed., *The Russian Military Into the Twenty-First Century* (London: Frank Cass, 2001), 75–93, citation 76.
19. *Novichkov, Snegovskii, and* Sokolov, *Rossiiskie vooruzhennye sily v chechnskom konflikte. Analiz, itogi, vyvody*, 102–105.
20. "Grachev, Grozny and Moscow snipers," *Jane's Defence Weekly*, January 21, 1995, 20.
21. Mariia Dement'yeva "Operatsiia po mozdoksko-arbatskim retseptam," *Segodnia*, February 15, 1995.
22. V. D. Solovei, "Voina v Chechne i rossiiskaia oppozitsiia," *Kentavr*, no. 5 (1995), 39–47.
23. Carlotta Gall and Thomas de Waal, *Chechnya: Calamity in the Caucasus* (New York: London, 1998), 161.
24. "Uroki chechenskogo krizisa. Spravka o razvitii sobytii vokrug Chechni, podgotovlennaia v Gosudarstvenno-pravovom Upravlenii Prezidenta Rossiiskoi Frderatsii," *Dialog*, no. 4 (1995), 34–38.
25. "Kavkazskaia voina," *Voennaia entsiklopediia*, vol. 9, K. I. Velichko, V. F. Novitskii, A. V. von Shwartz, V. A. Annushkin, and G. K. von Shultz, eds. (Spb., 1913), 220–242.
26. Pavel Fel'gengauer, "Operatsiia, kotoraia ne nravitsia nikomu," *Segodnia*, December 20, 1995.
27. Lester Grau, "Bashing the Laser Range Finder with a Rock," *Military Review*, 77, no. 3 (May–June 1997), 42–43, 44, 45–48.
28. Timothy Thomas, "Air Operations in Low Intensity Conflicts: The Case of Chechnya."
29. Stasys Knezys and Romanus Sedlickas, *The War in Chechnya* (College Station: Texas A&M University Press, 1998), 85–86.
30. Pavel Felgengauer, "Russian Campaign in Chechnya," e-version retrieved from www.amina.com/article.
31. Krasnaia zvezda, March 3, 1995.
32. Pavel Felgengauer, "Apocalypse now," *Segodnia*, January 5, 1995.
33. Novichkov, Snegovskii, and Sokolov, *Rossiiskie vooruzhennye sily v chechnskom konflikte. Analiz, itogi, vyvody*, 55.
34. Knezys and Sedlickas, *The War in Chechnya*, 114–115.
35. "Dudayev Talks on War in Chechnya," *The Baltic Observer*, March 30–April 5, 1995.
36. Charles Blandy, "The Battle for Grozny," *Jane's Intelligence Review*, 7, no. 2 (February 1995), 53–56.
37. Mariia Dement'eva and Mikhail Leont'ev, "Griaznaia voina protiv rossiiskoi armii," *Segodnia*, January 17, 1995.
38. *Krasnaia zvezda*, March 3, 1995.
39. Lieven, *Chechnya*, 127.
40. Vladimir Mukhin "Voennye uroki chechenskoi kampanii," Part 5, *Nezavisimoe voennoe obozrenie*, no. 22 (November 28, 1996), 2.
41. *Moskovskii komsomolets*, March 18, 1995.

42. Novichkov, Snegovskii, and Sokolov, *Rossiiskie vooruzhennye sily v chechnskom konflikte. Analiz, itogi, vyvody*, 75.
43. Ibid., 87.
44. Knezys and Sedlickas, *The War in Chechnya*, 179–185.
45. Mark Feigin, "Vtoraia kavkazskaia voina," *Novy mir*, no. 12 (1995), 159–171.
46. Pavel Fel'genauer, "Strana nevyuchennykh urokov," *Segodnia*, June 6, 1995.
47. Mark Galeotti, "Budyonnovsk and the Chechen War," *Jane's Intelligence Review*, 7, no. 8 (August 1995), 338.
48. "Kto ne khochet mira v Chechne," [interview with the Chief Public Relations Officer of the Federal Security Service Lieutenant General Aleksandr Mikhailov], *Novosti razvedki i kontrrazvedki*, nos. 15–16 (1995), 3; Knezys and Sedlickas, *The War in Chechnya*, 173; Lieven, *Chechnya*, 124.
49. "Terroristy pronikaiut v Rossiiu za den'gi," [interview with Shamil' Basaev], *Nezavisimaia gazeta*, March 12, 1996.
50. Anjei Lomanovski, "V gorakh u chechenskikh partzan," *Novoe vremia*, no. 28 (1995), 10–11.
51. Pavel Grachev, "Stavka na silu v Chechne dolzhna byt' sokhranena," [interview], *Nezavisimoe voennoe obozrenie*, no. 3 (November 1995), 1–2.
52. Mikhail Korovkin and Aleksei Nemenov, "Poslednii boi? Bamutskaia operatsiia kak zerkalo chechenskoi voiny," *Itogi*, July 4, 1996, 15–17.
53. Vladimir Semiriaga, "Chto delaiut pogranvoiska v Chechne," *Novosti razvedki i kontrrazvedki*, no. 4 (1996), 3.
54. Valentin Aleksandrov, "Sud'ba Chechni posle vtoroi kavkazskoi voiny," *Nezavisimaia gazeta*, March 14, 1996.
55. Iusup Soslambekov, "Piatyi genotsid," *Novoe vremia*, no. 4 (1996), 10–12.
56. Konstantin Petrov, "Neprimirimye na trope voiny," *Orientir*, no. 6 (1996), 11–12.
57. Gregory J. Calestan, "Wounded Bear: The Ongoing Russian Military Operation in Chechnya," e-version retrieved from www.amina.com/article/mil_oper.html.
58. Galina Koval'skaia, Aleksandr Iskanderian, "Poiski mira po zakonam voiny," *Novoe vremia*, no. 14 (1996), 8–10.
59. Il'ia Maksakov, "Boi v Groznom. Mnozhatsia bessmyslennye zhertvy," *Nezavisimaia gazeta*, March 12, 1996.
60. Vladimir Mukhin, "Voennye uroki chechenskoi kampanii," Part 7, *Nezavisimoe voennoe obozrenie*, no. 1 (January 11–18, 1997), 2.
61. "Pervomaiskoe. Ekho operatsii" [press conference of the Army General Mikhail Barsukov], *Novosti razvedki i kontrrazvedki*, no. 3 (1996), 4–5.
62. Galina Koval'skaia, "Kapituliatsii ne budet," *Itogi*, June 4, 1996, 10–12.
63. Gall and de Waal, *Chechnya*, 331.
64. Vladimir Mukhin, "Voennye uroki chechenskoi kampanii," Part 8, *Nezavisimoe voennoe obozrenie*, no. 3 (January 25–30, 1997), 2; Gall and de Waal, *Chechnya*, 332.
65. "Grozny–zharkii avgust-96," *Novosti razvedki i kontrazvedki*, no. 17 (1996), 8–10.
66. "Krovavyi avgust," *Vainakh*, no. 2 (1996/1997), 20–25.
67. "Russia resumes fighting despite election pledge," *Jane's Defence Weekly*, August 14, 1996, 4.

68. Nikolai Astashkin, "Uzhe deistvuiut shturmovye grupy desantnikov i motostrelkov," *Krasnaia zvezda*, August 13, 1996.
69. Knezys and Sedlickas, *The War in Chechnya*, 293–294.
70. Galina Koval'skaia, "Tonkii led chechnskogo mira," *Itogi*, September 24, 1996, 12–15.
71. Aslan Maskhadov, "My khotim byt' sub'ektami mezhdunarodnogo prava. . . ," (interview), *Novoe vremia*, no. 38 (1996), 6–8.
72. Timothy Thomas, "Air Operations in Low Intensity Conflicts," passim.
73. Pavel Fel'gengauer, "U chechentsev net sistemy PVO, kak takovoi," *Segodnia*, February 3, 1995.
74. Novichkov, Snegovskii, and Sokolov, *Rossiiskie vooruzhennye sily v chechnskom konflikte. Analiz, itogi, vyvody*, 115.
75. Knezys and Sedlickas, *The War in Chechnya*, 76–78.
76. Novichkov, Snegovskii, and Sokolov, *Rossiiskie vooruzhennye sily v chechnskom konflikte. Analiz, itogi, vyvody*, 51.
77. Lieven, *Chechnya*, 114.
78. Nataliia Gorodetskaia, "Rossiiskie voiska nachali bombardirovku Gudermesa," *Segodnia*, February 3, 1995.
79. Knezys and Sedlickas, *The War in Chechnya*, 104–105.
80. Vladimir Mukhin, "Voennye uroki chechenskoi kampanii," Part 8, *Nezavisimoe voennoe obozrenie*, no. 3 (January 25–30, 1997), 2.
81. For detail see Lester Grau, "Russian Manufactured Armored Vehicle Vulnerability in Urban Combat: The Chechen Experience," e-version retrieved from www.amina.com/article/mil; Novichkov, Snegovskii, and Sokolov, *Rossiiskie vooruzhennye sily v chechnskom konflikte. Analiz, itogi, vyvody*, 138–147.
82. Aleksandr Kostiuchenko, "Uroki Groznogo," *Armeiskii sbornik*, no. 11 (1995), 29–30.
83. Natal'ia Gorodetskaia, "Federal'nye voiska poluchaiut podkreplenie," *Segodnia*, January 17, 1995.
84. "Pamiatka lichnomu sostavu chastei i podrazdelenii po vedeniiu boevykh deistvii v Chechenskoi respublike," *Armeiskii sbornik*, no. 1 (1996), 37–42.
85. Pavel Fel'gengauer, "Rossiiskaia armiia primeniaet novuiu taktiku," *Segodnia*, January 10, 1995.
86. Aleksandr Yevtukhov, "S popravkoi na boevoi opyt," *Orientir*, no. 9 (1995), 35–39.
87. Lester Grau, "Russian Urban Tactics. Lessons from the Battle for Grozny," *Strategic Forum*, INSS, no. 38 (July 1995); Vladimir Suzda'tsev, "Chechenskie uroki voiskovoi PVO," *Armeiskii sbornik*, no. 9 (1995), 23–25.
88. Oleg Namsaraev, "Prochesyvanie naselennykh punktov," *Armeiskii sbornik*, no. 4 (1995), 35–37.
89. Lieven, *Chechnya*, 116.
90. A. A. Korabel'nikov and A. V. Chernenko, "Taktika deistvii partizanskikh formirovanii v tylu protivnika," *Voennaia mysl'*, no. 2 (January–February 1997), 36–42.
91. Gall and de Waal, *Chechnya*, 289–317.
92. Knezys and Sedlickas, *The War in Chechnya*, 174.
93. Vitalii Tret'iakov, "Dudayev dobil Chechniu," *Nezavisimaia gazeta*, January 18, 1996.
94. Oleg Blotskii, "Zapadnia sredi razvalin," *Nezavisimoe voennoe obozrenie*, no. 6 (March 28, 1996), 2.

95. Nikolai Kovalev, "Avtotekhnika v chechenskom konflikte," *Armeiskii sbornik*, no. 3 (1996), 62–64.

96. Andrei Levin, "Voennaia razvedka v Chechne. Proschety i uroki," *Novosti razvedki i kontrrazvedki*, no. 18 (1996), 7.

97. Novichkov, Snegovskii, and Sokolov, *Rossiiskie vooruzhennye sily v chechnskom konflikte. Analiz, itogi, vyvody*, 113.

98. Yevgenii Krutikov, "Kadrovyi nokdaun," *Novoe vremia*, no. 26 (1996), 20–21.

99. Timothy L. Thomas, *Caucasus Conflict and Russian Security: The Russian Armed Forces Confront Chechnya* (Fort Leavenworth, KS: Foreign Military Studies Office, 1995), 41.

100. Novichkov, Snegovskii, and Sokolov, *Rossiiskie vooruzhennye sily v chechnskom konflikte. Analiz, itogi, vyvody*, 106.

101. Aleksandr Cherkasov, "Kliuch k pobede," *Orientir*, no. 9 (1996), 16–19.

102. See Wayne Masden, "Did NSA Help Russia Target Dudayev?" *Covert Action Quarterly*, no. 61 (1997), 47–49; "Kak pogib Dzhokhar Dudayev?" *Novosti razvedki i kontrrazvedki*, no. 18 (1997), 3.

103. Timothy Thomas, "Air Operations in Low Intensity Conflicts," passim.

104. Sergei Grigoriev, "Chechenskaia operatsiia v svete ei podobnykh," *Nezavisimaia gazeta* (June 21, 1995).

105. Voennye reformy v Rosii, *Materialy konferentsii* (March 1997), 56–57.

106. V.A. Vakhrushev, "Lokal'nye voiny i vooruzhennye konflikty. Kharakter I vliianie na voennoe iskusstvo," *Voennaia mysl'*, no. 4 (July–August 1999), 20–28.

107. Vladimir Kadetov, "Spetsial'nye operatsii vooruzhennykh sil," *Nezavisimoe voennoe obozrenie*, no. 23 (December 26, 1996), 2.

108. Dmitrii Yestaf'ev, "Operatsiia v Chechne kak paradigma vooruzhennogo konflikta postsovetskogo perioda," *Problemy vneshnei i oboronnoi politiki Rossii*, no. 3 (1995), 57–84.

109. D. A. Prikhozhii, "Ob upravlenii gruppirovkami voisk v khode vooruzhennykh konfliktov," *Voennaia mysl'*, no. 4 (July–August 1999)

110. I. N. Vorob'ev, "Vzaimodeistvie silovykh struktur v vooruzhennom konflikte," *Voennaia mysl'*, no. 6 (November–December 1999), 45–49.

111. V. N. Maganov, "Formy i sposoby primeneniia gruppirovok voisk (sil) v vooruzhennykh konfliktakh," *Voennaia mysl'*, no. 2 (March–April 1996).

112. Iurii Tuchkov, "Ob'edinennye gruppirovki voisk I formy ikh primeneniia v vooruzhennykh konfliktakh i lokal'nykh voinakh," *Voennaia mysl'*, no. 2 (March–April 1997), 30–5.

113. A. N. Khaev, N. V. Smolkotin, and I. F. Danilin, "Sistema sil spetsial'nogo naznacheniia. Trebovaniia i svoistva," *Voennaia mysl'*, no. 6 (November–December 1999), 25–28.

114. M. I. Karatuev and V.A. Dreschuk, "Osobennosti boevogo primeneniia artillerii v lokal'nykh voinakh i vooruzhennykh konfliktakh," *Voennaia mysl'*, no. 3 (May–June 1995), 22–28.

115. V. S. Pirumov and M. A. Rodionov, "Nekotorye aspekty informatsionnoi bor'by v vooruzhennykh konfliktakh," *Voennaia mysl'*, no. 5 (September–October 1996), 45–48.

116. Aleksandr Shirokorad, "'Nona' nesravnennaia," *Voin*, no. 12 (1999), 95–97.

117. Anatolii Obukhov, "Anti-Tank Grenade. Weapons of the 21st Century," issue 35, (September–October, 1999), e-version retrieved from www.milparade.com.

118. Mikhail Zakharchuk, "Uroki chechenskogo krizisa," *Armeiskii sbornik*, no. 4 (1995), 44–46.
119. Ralph Peters, "The Future of Armored Warfare," *Parameters*, vol. 27, no. 3 (Summer 1997), 50, 51, 52–59.

Chapter 7: Conclusion

1. Dale R. Herspring, "Putin and the Armed Forces," ch. 8 in Herspring, ed., *Putin's Russia: Past Imperfect, Future Uncertain* (Lanham, MD: Rowman and Littlefield, 2003), 155–175.
2. As James M. Goldgeier and Michael McFaul have noted, "In foreign affairs, the main story of the 1990s was the breathtaking speed with which Russia declined as a major power." See Goldgeier and McFaul, *Power and Purpose: U.S. Policy toward Russia after the Cold War* (Washington, DC: Brookings Institution, 2003), 359 and passim.
3. *USA Today*, February 27, 2002, A1, and passim.
4. Stephen J. Blank, "Potemkin's Treadmill: Russian Military Modernization," in Ashley J. Tellis and Michael Wills, eds., *Strategic Asia 2005–06: Military Modernization in an Age of Uncertainty* (Washington, DC: National Bureau of Asian Research, 2005), 175–205, citation on page 177.
5. Ibid.
6. A considerable literature documents this point. See, for example: Pavel K. Baev, "The Trajectory of the Russian Military: Downsizing, Degeneration, and Defeat," ch. 1, 43–72; and Alexei G. Arbatov, "Military Reform: From Crisis to Stagnation," ch. 3, 95–120, both in Steven E. Miller and Dmitri V. Trenin, eds., *The Russian Military: Power and Policy* (Cambridge, MA: MIT Press, 2004).

INDEX

1,700 warhead limit: U.S. and Russian performance under, 78–80, *79*; U.S. and Russian strategic nuclear forces at, 69–73, 91–93; U.S. and Russian surviving and penetrating warheads at, 85–86, *86*; U.S. and Russian surviving and retaliating warheads at, *60*

2,200 warhead limit: U.S. and Russian performance under, 78–80, *79*; U.S. and Russian strategic nuclear forces at, 65–69, 91–93; U.S. and Russian surviving and penetrating warheads at, *85*, 85–86; U.S. and Russian surviving and retaliating warheads at, *59*

ABMs. *See* antiballistic missile systems
ABM Treaty, 16, 32–33, 75
absolutism, renunciation of, 136
accidental war, prevention of, 37
accidents, normal, 51–52
Afghanistan: Soviet Union and, 40, 146; U.S. operations in, 16, 20–21, 43
Afghan syndrome, 116
air defense, in Chechen War, 118, 126
air-launched cruise missiles (ALCMs), 77
Allied Force, Operation, 43
al Qaeda, 16
Andropov, Yuri, 40
antiballistic missile systems (ABM), 82
Argun-Gudermes-Shali Operation, 122
arms control, missile defense and, 82–90
Army of the Potomac Cavalry Corps, 48–49

atomic weapons. *See* nuclear weapons
attack assessment, 50–52; errors in, types of, 51
authority: delegation of, 52–56; in U.S. versus Russian systems, 55
authorization, definition of, 53

Babichev, Ivan, 120
Baku-Novorossiisk pipeline, 114
ballistic missile defenses (BMD), 31–32; critics of, 82; Gorbachev and, 41
ballistic missile early warning radars (BMEWS), 50
ballistic missile submarines (SSBNs), 76; communication with, 48–49
Barbarossa, Operation, 1–11; lessons from, 10–11; Soviet force structure in, *5*; timing of, 3
Basaev, Shamil', 122–23
Betts, Richard K., 9
biases, types of, 48
Blair, Bruce G., 56–57, 60
Blank, Stephen J., viii
Bloch, Ivan, 110
BMD. *See* ballistic missile defenses
BMEWS. *See* ballistic missile early warning radars
bomber pilots, training of, 57
bombers: Moscow Treaty on, 76–77; Soviet and American levels of, *34*
boost phase intercept technology, 87
Bracken, Paul, 52
Brezhnev, Leonid, 25, 31, 41, 146
Budenny, S. M., 4–5
Budyonnovsk, 122
Bush, George W., 16, 75, 80, 100, 106–7

ABOUT THE AUTHORS

STEPHEN J. CIMBALA is an award–winning teacher and Distinguished Professor of Political Science at Penn State University (Delaware County) who has written extensively about national security policy, nuclear arms control, and defense affairs. Cimbala's most recent book is *Nuclear Weapons and Strategy*. He has served as an adviser or consultant to several U.S. government agencies and think tanks. He lives in Drexel Hill, Pennsylvania.

PETER JACOB RAINOW is a defense consultant and author or co-author of five books on security issues. In 1991–1992, he participated in the Consensus Project on the future of U.S.–Russia relations at the John M. Olin Institute of Strategic Studies, Harvard University. He was a visiting scholar at Stanford University in 1996–1997. Rainow lives in Foster City, California.